boutique
bead&wire
jewelry

boutique
bead&wire
jewelry

Melody MacDuffee

LARK BOOKS
A Division of Sterling Publishing Co., Inc.
New York / London

SENIOR EDITOR
▶ Marthe Le Van

EDITOR
▶ Larry Shea

ART DIRECTOR
▶ Megan Kirby

COVER DESIGNER
▶ Cindy LaBreacht

ILLUSTRATOR
▶ J'aime Allene

PHOTOGRAPHERS
▶ Stewart O'Shields,
   Steve Mann

Library of Congress Cataloging-in-Publication Data

MacDuffee, Melody.
  Boutique bead & wire jewelry / Melody MacDuffee. -- 1st ed.
    p. cm.
  Includes index.
  ISBN-13: 978-1-60059-094-8 (pb-trade pbk. : alk. paper)
  ISBN-10: 1-60059-094-2 (pb-trade pbk. : alk. paper)
  1. Jewelry making. 2. Wire jewelry. 3. Beadwork. I. Title. II. Title:
Boutique bead and wire jewelry.
  TT212.M26 2008
  739.27--dc22

                                    2007046539

10 9 8 7 6 5 4 3 2 1

First Edition

Published by Lark Books, A Division of
Sterling Publishing Co., Inc.
387 Park Avenue South, New York, NY 10016

Text © 2008, Melody MacDuffee
Photos and illustrations © 2008, Lark Books

Distributed in Canada by Sterling Publishing,
c/o Canadian Manda Group, 165 Dufferin Street
Toronto, Ontario, Canada M6K 3H6

Distributed in the United Kingdom by GMC Distribution Services,
Castle Place, 166 High Street, Lewes, East Sussex, England BN7 1XU

Distributed in Australia by Capricorn Link (Australia) Pty Ltd.,
P.O. Box 704, Windsor, NSW 2756 Australia

If you have questions or comments about this book, please contact:
Lark Books
67 Broadway
Asheville, NC 28801
828-253-0467

44946753 2/11

Manufactured in China

For information about custom editions, special sales, premium and corpo-
rate purchases, please contact Sterling Special Sales Department at
800-805-5489 or specialsales@sterlingpub.com

DEDICATION

▶ To the women of Knot Just Beads,
who unceasingly teach, challenge,
support, and inspire me.

boutique
bead & wire
jewelry

introduction

WHAT DRAWS STUDENTS TO MY CLASSES IN MAKING JEWELRY WITH BEADS AND TWISTED WIRE? IT'S DEFINITELY THE END RESULT.
The pieces of jewelry look so classic, they tell me. Delicate. Intricate. And sparkly! To them, this jewelry looks like the kind they might stumble across in a smart little boutique, and happily scoop up to take home and add to their collection.

But they also think it looks complex. Hard to make. And a real challenge, especially for those with little or no experience in making jewelry. The secret my students learn by the end of a single three-hour class—and one you'll discover in this book—is how twisted wire is such a fun technique to work with, and one that is surprisingly easy to master. Within the first half hour, my students begin to relax as they see their pieces already taking shape. A few hours later, they've surprised themselves by completing a one-of-a-kind showpiece necklace, bracelet, or fancy pair of earrings. Nearly all feel confident enough to go forward on their own to design jewelry that is not only beautiful, but utterly unique.

The pieces of bead and wire jewelry in this book might look like ones you'd only find in a store featuring the work of accomplished jewelry makers. Luckily, the technique for creating them is actually quite simple. It consists of twisting two lengths of fine-gauge wire together, and adding beads at regular or irregular intervals in an unlimited variety of configurations. Twisting longer stems and branches produces a lacy, airy look. Keeping the stems and branches shorter brings the motifs closer together, creating a lusher appearance. In either

case, the results are spectacular, with gracefully twining filigree effects.

The twisting process, when done correctly, strengthens the wires, which would otherwise be too delicate to bear the weight of the beaded motifs. In some pieces, the filigrees are framed within carefully molded lengths of thicker, less flexible wire, which serves to stabilize them and make them even stronger.

Besides the simplicity of the techniques used, one great aspect of this type of jewelry—as you'll learn in the Basics section that follows—is how easy it is to get all the necessary tools and materials. The list of essential tools has only three items on it: two types of pliers and a pair of wire cutters. Add one or two spools of wire and a few selections from the wide and glorious world of beads, and you're ready to go.

After a discussion of tools and materials, the Basics section goes on to give you all the tips and tricks you'll need to start, add onto, and finish the pieces in the book. The last section before the projects—one you'll refer back to often—is called the Motif Boutique. These bead and wire motifs are the building blocks you put together in endless combinations to make your own unique pieces.

When you move on to the varied jewelry projects that follow, you'll discover one reason why this twisted wire technique is so relaxing to do. It's *really* difficult to make a mistake. Irregularities that might look like mistakes at first can nearly always be "tweaked" later into shapes that enhance the beauty of the piece. A section of "stem" that was made too long can be looped around, bringing the motifs on either side of it closer together while

adding an attractive flourish. A spindly-looking "branch" can be gracefully curved and re-curved to fill in a sparse section of a necklace or bracelet.

This "fixibility" is important to remember as you follow the patterns in this book. I have provided measurements for all the stems and branches, but as guidelines only. With very few exceptions, any of the pieces here would not have been adversely affected had I made some stems longer or some branches shorter. They might have looked a little bit different, but not worse—possibly even better!

So relax and have fun with the technique, secure in the knowledge that a good tweaking session at the end of your efforts will take care of any awkward angles or inelegant curves. Twist away, and then enjoy the oohs and aahs from friends and relatives when you wear your new creations. When they ask for the name of the shop where you bought them, they'll be stunned when you tell them you made them yourself. Just don't let slip how easy and fun it was to do.

frame wires

Some of the advanced projects in this book call for stiffer wires to be used as frames to which filigrees are attached. Use either of two types:

- Half-hard sterling or gold-fill wire in 20-gauge.

- Memory wire. This base metal wire is even stiffer than half-hard wire. While it's designed to "remember" its original shape, you can mold it to a certain extent and bend it using flat-nose pliers. You can find it in gold look and sterling silver look as well as in silvery gray. It comes in choker, bracelet, and ring shapes.

◀ Memory wire

▶ **A word of warning: Don't use your regular wire cutters on memory wire—the wire will nick the blades and ruin the cutters.**

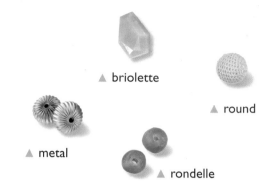

▲ briolette

▲ round

▲ metal

▲ rondelle

▲ Assorted beads

beads

When combining beads with twisted wire jewelry, it's best to stick with beads that measure 6 mm or less (and 4 mm or less for smaller and more delicate pieces). Heavy beads will weigh down the wire and cause your jewelry to sag or lose its shape. If you do want to use larger beads, consider using a 26-gauge wire.

You can use almost any shape of small bead, including seed beads. Glass, plastic, crystal, and stone all work well. Be careful when selecting metal beads, though, as some may be too heavy.

For the "petal" beads of flower shapes, choose small rondelles, bicones, round beads, or briolettes (small teardrop-shaped beads that are drilled across their tips). Stay away from teardrop beads that are drilled from top to bottom and also from oval beads that are drilled lengthwise, such as fire-polished crystals. These can work fine for other parts of the designs—just not for the petals.

▲ Seed beads

▲ Bicone crystal beads

▲ Findings

findings and other materials

You can find the clasps, ear wires, headbands, and other pre-made pieces you'll need for various projects at any large craft store or through a jewelry-supply catalog. Almost all findings work well with twisted wire jewelry. Feel free to make substitutions (toggles for lobster claws, posts for fish hooks, etc.) when creating your pieces.

The only other material that you may need is a good epoxy glue.

working with wires & beads

The primary technique for every project in this book is a simple one: twist two wires together to form a "main stem," then detour at regular or irregular intervals to add "branches" that end in single-bead or multiple-bead motifs. Motifs are standard patterns of twists and beads (a five-petal flower, for example) that appear and repeat throughout the book's projects. You'll find an illustrated guide to making all the motifs on page 30. The twisting process is not only decorative, it also strengthens your wire, lending durability to your piece.

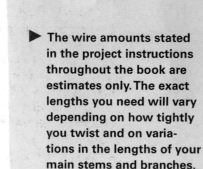

▶ The wire amounts stated in the project instructions throughout the book are estimates only. The exact lengths you need will vary depending on how tightly you twist and on variations in the lengths of your main stems and branches.

getting started

How do you begin a piece of twisted wire jewelry? Choose one of three methods.

1. beginning with a motif

This is the easiest way to begin a piece. A motif, such as a flower or a leaf, gives you something substantial to hold on to when you begin the first twisted portion of your piece, allowing for better control of the twisting process. The Motif Boutique, page 000, shows you how to create all the motifs used in this book. Here's how to use a motif to start any piece:

a. Cut the length of wire called for in the instructions.

b. Add the specified beads, and slide them to the halfway point of your wire (see photo 1).

c. Follow the instructions in the Motif Dictionary for the motif you're making.

▲ photo 1

2. beginning with a loop

You can also begin a piece with a loop, then attach something (an ear wire, for example) later.

a. Cut the length of wire called for in the instructions, and fold it in half.

b. Hold the two sections of wire slightly apart, just far enough down from the center so you can insert the tip of your pliers into the opening (see photo 2).

c. Give the pliers three half-twists.

◀ photo 2

3. beginning with two pieces of wire

A few projects begin by simply twisting two pieces of wire together.

a. Cut the length of wire called for in the instructions.

b. Hold the two wires just slightly apart, an inch or two (2.5 to 5 cm) from one end (see photo 3). Twist the wires with the hand farther from the end, backing away bit by bit as you twist, until you reach the length called for in the instructions.

◀ photo 3

securing a motif or loop of beads in place

However you begin a piece, you'll have to make your motif or loop secure. Cross your wires at the base, holding them close up against the beads or loop between your thumb and forefinger, so the loop is snug. Wrap the working end of your wire around the other very tightly twice, right up against the base of the loop (see photo 4).

◀ photo 4

▶ **For the sake of brevity (and with apologies to left-handed readers), instructions that require explanations in terms of which hand to use for a task have been explained in right-handed terms. If you're left-handed, simply substitute "right" for "left" and vice versa in those cases.**

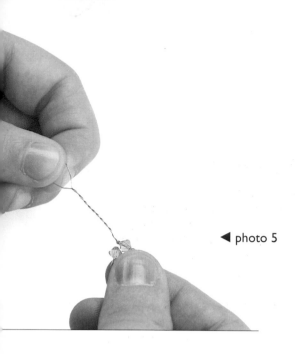

◀ photo 5

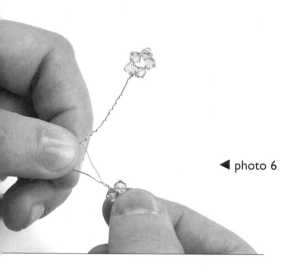

◀ photo 6

◀ photo 7

twisting main stems & branches

Any time you twist your two main wires together, you're creating a section of "main stem" (see photo 5). If you're using only one of your wires—leaving the other dormant as you fold your working wire over, make a motif, and twist the two sections of this working wire together back to the main stem—then you're making a "branch" (see photo 6). The basic technique for twisting stems and branches is the same.

Here are the simple steps for achieving a nice, even twist.

1. Hold your two wires just slightly apart (⅛ inch [3 mm] or so) between the thumb and forefinger of your left hand near the point where your twisted section of stem or branch is to begin.

2. Hold the motif (or the two wires, if you're beginning a main stem with two pieces of wire rather than a motif or loop) between the thumb and forefinger of your right hand, and twist it several times.

3. Begin backing your left hand away from this twisted portion bit by bit, about ⅛ to ¼ inch (3 to 6 mm) at a time, still holding your two wires just slightly apart between the thumb and forefinger of your left hand as you continue to twist with your right hand (see photo 7).

4. Stop when you've twisted the length of stem or branch called for in the pattern.

Over-twisting will cause your wire to become brittle and easily breakable. Under-twising will make your piece flabby and weak. Aim to achieve the look in photo 7, which is just right.

▶ **Get used to always twisting your motifs in the same direction (either away from you or toward you). This way, if you need to correct something down the road, you will know which way to untwist.**

troubleshooting your twisting technique

1. If your twisted portion looks as if one wire is wrapped around the other, one of two things is probably happening:

- You may be twisting the wires instead of twisting the motif. Always hold the wires steady and twist the motif.

- You may not be holding the wires apart with your left hand as you twist with your right. Holding them just slightly apart keeps the individual wires from twisting around between your fingers; this gives you greater control of the whole process.

2. If you're having trouble controlling the length of your twisted sections, try the following:

- If your wire seems to want to twist past the point where you intended it to stop, try pressing the wires more tightly between the thumb and forefinger of your left hand, bearing down with your thumbnail at the exact point where you want the twisted portion to end.

- If you're making a branch and having trouble securing your motif at the correct distance from your main stem, try pressing down with your thumbnail on your working wire just below the bottom bead of your motif, right at the point that marks the correct distance, before making your initial loop of beads and securing the motif.

▶ tweaking

If you're concerned your piece looks stiff and awkward as you're making it, don't worry—this is normal. As long as the proportions are somewhere in the right ballpark, you can take care of the problem when you tweak and shape the piece later on. Compare pieces A and B in photo 8 for an example of how tweaking wires can make a big difference in the final result of your pieces. For more help, see Tweaking & Shaping, page 22.

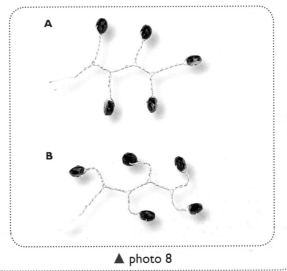

▲ photo 8

dealing with kinks in your wire

If your wire is kinking, try these suggestions:

1. Because wire usually comes on spools or in coils, it will naturally tend to curl. Uncurl it from time to time by slowly pulling the wire between the thumb and forefinger of one hand while holding it with the other. Be careful not to cause kinks to occur as you do this—the curls can close up into kinks if you're not vigilant. But in general, kinks are less likely to occur when the wire is less curly.

2. If you see a kink forming in your wire, don't pull it tight. If you catch it early enough, while it's still actually a small loop, you can sometimes gently turn the wire at that point to undo the loop.

3. If you get a full-blown kink in your wire, you can sometimes press it out with flat-nose pliers. You'll probably have to press it from several angles before it will feel smooth enough to slide easily as you work with it.

4. As a last resort, you may have to cut the wire just above the kink and resign yourself to having to add in new wire (see the next section) sooner than you otherwise would have.

adding new wire

Sometimes, the total length of wire a piece requires would just be too much to control effectively from the start. At other times, you may accidentally break your wire or have to cut it because of a kink. In either case, you'll have to add new wire. The trick is to learn how to do this without leaving an overly noticeable clump of wire where the old one ends and the new one begins.

attaching a new wire to a motif

This is the best—and least noticeable—place to add in new wire.

1. Cut your new wire and fold it in half.

2. Place the fold across the twisted section at the base of your motif (see photo 9).

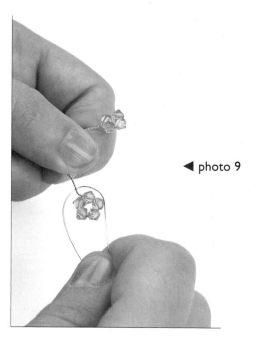

◀ photo 9

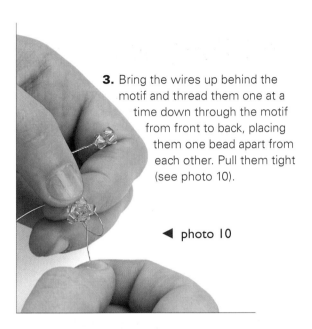

3. Bring the wires up behind the motif and thread them one at a time down through the motif from front to back, placing them one bead apart from each other. Pull them tight (see photo 10).

◀ photo 10

4. Repeat step C from "thread them one at a time…" You should be able to hold the piece by the new wires without it flopping down as if it were hinged. If you cannot, thread the wires through the motif again, changing the locations of the wires a bit, if necessary, to make the "join" more stable.

5. Flip the piece around so you can continue twisting the next section according to your pattern instructions (see photo 11).

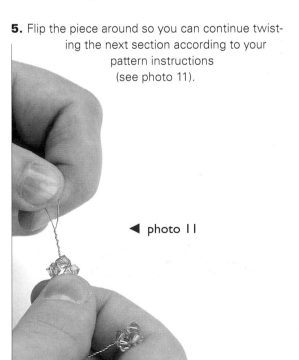

◀ photo 11

attaching a new wire to a branch or stem ending

If you can't add new wire at a motif—if it would disturb your pattern, for example—then the next best place to add it is at a fork, where a branch meets your main stem.

1. Cut your new wire and fold it in half.

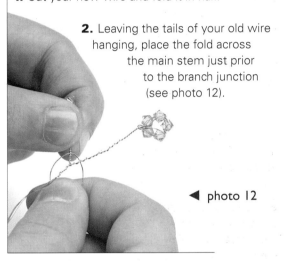

2. Leaving the tails of your old wire hanging, place the fold across the main stem just prior to the branch junction (see photo 12).

◀ photo 12

3. Tightly wrap up one end of the new wire once or twice from behind and around the stem just prior to the branch junction, keeping the wraps as close to it as possible. Wrap up the other end from behind and around the branch in the same manner (see photo 13). The extra layer of new wire will be less noticeable if you align your wraps with the pattern of twisting already there.

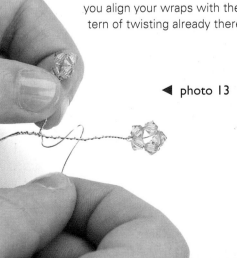

◀ photo 13

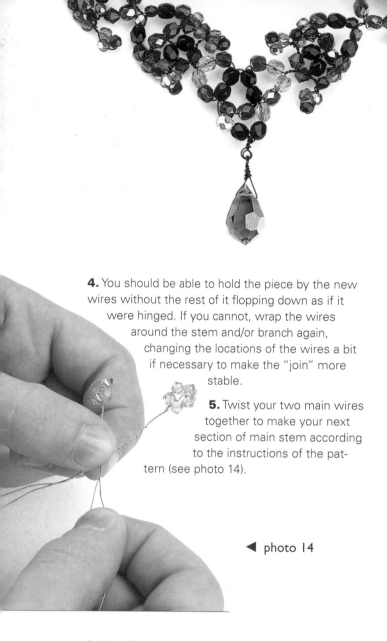

4. You should be able to hold the piece by the new wires without the rest of it flopping down as if it were hinged. If you cannot, wrap the wires around the stem and/or branch again, changing the locations of the wires a bit if necessary to make the "join" more stable.

5. Twist your two main wires together to make your next section of main stem according to the instructions of the pattern (see photo 14).

◀ photo 14

6. Untwist the portion of your main stem (if any) that lies after the branch junction all the way back to the stem junction. Then twist each of the old wire tails around your new section of main stem in the same manner as above.

7. Clip all tails and press them down as explained in Finishing Off Your Wires (page 21). Press all the wraps you've just made to minimize any clumping effect.

8. Continue according to the project instructions.

adding new wire to a frame

Some projects require a wire frame for greater stability. If you run out of wire when attaching a twisted wire filigree to a frame, simply wrap the old wire two or three times around the frame. Then position one end of your new wire beside the old one, making sure that when you continue with the new wire, you're wrapping in the same direction as before. Wrap the new wire around the frame several times, and continue working your piece as usual.

If you run out of wire when you're ready to begin wrapping into the filigree to attach it to the frame, back up a few wraps, add the new wire as above, and then attach the filigree.

finishing off your wires

When you're done with a piece of wire, whether because you've finished a section or because you're ready to add new wire in, you must anchor the ends of the old wires, clip the tails, and press them down so there will be no sharp ends sticking out on your finished piece. Here are three procedures to follow.

1. anchoring your old wires

Anchoring is done by wrapping tails of the old wires around the nearest available section of stem, branch, motif, or frame, taking care to choose the spots where the added bulk of these wraps will be least obvious.

2. clipping the tails

Always cut the tails off at the front side of your piece (especially when making necklaces and bracelets) so there's no possibility of stray rough wire ends pricking skin.

Sometimes you'll be forced by the density of wires and/or motifs in the area where you are clipping to go in with the point of your cutters. Otherwise, always clip your wires by placing the back side of your cutters (the side flush with the blade) right up against the stem, branch, motif, or frame the wires are wrapped around.

3. pressing the tails

Always press the clipped tails down with your flat-nose pliers, rotating them gently in the same direction that the wires were being twisted or wrapped. Then run your fingers across the area to check for sharp ends. If you find some, keep pressing them down and/or clip them a bit more.

▶ **When you're finishing wires, it's essential to use wire cutters that are fairly small, sharp, and come to a fine point (like the pair shown on page 10).**

tweaking & shaping

Most pieces of twisted wire jewelry look quite stiff and awkward until they've been nudged into more balanced shapes and their stems and branches have been "tweaked" into more graceful curves and angles.

In some cases, it's okay to tweak your stems and branches every so often to get a better idea of how a piece will look in the end. But if you're making two pieces that must match (such as earrings) or a necklace or bracelet that must be worked outward from the center point with the two sides mirroring each other, it's best to wait to tweak until after you've twisted both pieces. That way you can use the pre-tweaked version as a guide as you try to replicate its proportions.

In advanced projects, when you're trying to fit twisted-wire filigree around or into a frame, more extensive tweaking may be necessary to get the filigree's points of contact to line up with the shape of the frame. This will take a bit of negotiating, so be patient. Just keep curling the branches in closer to the main stem so that their outer motifs line up against the edges of the frame.

tweaking

Tweaking is done by using round-nose pliers to curve, curl, and loop stems and branches so they twine gracefully instead of sticking straight out. The process also gives you a chance to rearrange the placement of motifs to a certain extent, so they're more evenly and attractively distributed throughout a piece, filling in any gaps and thinning out too-crowded areas. Here are some techniques you can use.

1. To give a branch a more graceful, curving shape and/or to bring its motif closer in toward your main stem, grip it with round-nose pliers near its motif and roll the pliers sideways. If this moves the motif too far to one side or the other, grip the branch down close to the stem and nudge the bottom part of the branch in the opposite direction, so it lies more nearly parallel to the main stem.

2. If a branch is particularly long, giving it a spindly look, you can curl a loop or a loop plus a curve somewhere along its length (see examples **A**, **B**, and **C** in photo 15). Or give it an "S" curve (see example **D**). These tweaks not only bring the motif in toward the main stem, but also fill in unwanted space that might be making the area seem sparse.

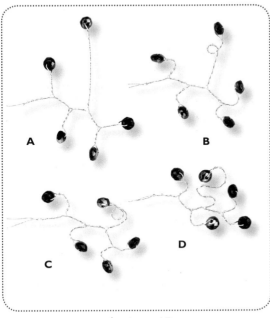

▲ photo 15

3. If you have too much main stem space be-tween branches, you can do to the stem all the same things that work for long branches (see examples **E**, **F**, and **G** in photo 16).

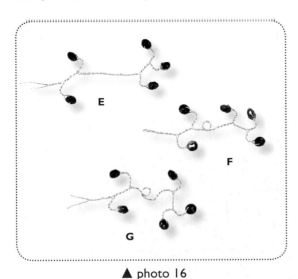

▲ photo 16

4. If an area on one side of your main stem is too crowded and the other side too sparse, simply flip one of the branches to the stem's other side. Be-gin by giving the whole main stem a half twist in the direction you originally twisted it, right before the branch. Then give the stem another half twist just after the branch—this will return everything else to where it was before you tweaked (see examples **H**, **I**, and **J** in photo 17).

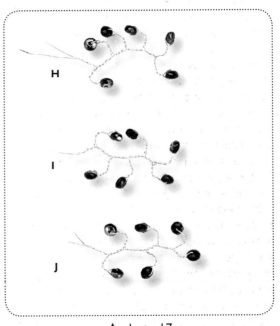

▲ photo 17

shaping

Once you've tweaked to your satisfaction, a piece may still need some general shaping, particularly in the case of necklaces that must conform to the shape of a neck. Most shaping can be done without pliers, just by nudging the main stem with your fingers a little bit at a time until the piece lies attractively and comfortably when worn.

adding clasps & ear wires

To add a clasp or ear wire, finish the decorative portions of your piece first (unless the project's instructions say otherwise), but don't finish off your wires. Instead, twist them together to make another inch or two (2.5 to 5 cm) of main stem, and clip the tails. Thread this main stem portion through the loop on your clasp or ear wire. Checking for the desired length of the finished piece, position the clasp or ear wire accordingly and fold the tail end of the main stem back. Holding your two twisted portions (the tail and the part just before the fold) just slightly apart with your left hand, twist the clasp or ear wire four or five times, just as you would twist the wires of a branch after making its motif. Finish off your wires as explained on page 21.

wire wrapping

Some of the projects call for traditional wire wraps. To make them, simply follow the steps for the simple wire-wrapped loop or the hanger-style wire-wrapped loop.

simple wire-wrapped loop

1. Grip the wire(s) with your round-nose pliers just below the point where you want your loop to be, and bend the wire with your thumb to form a 90-degree angle (see photo 18).

◄ photo 18

2. Holding your piece so that the stem section prior to the bend is vertical and the bent portion is horizontal, reposition your pliers so that they are gripping the horizontal portion right up against the vertical stem (see photo 19). Using the round shape of your pliers to shape the loop, wrap the horizontal portion up and over around the top rung of the pliers and then on around to make a full circle, making sure that you are going around only one rung of the pliers at any time so that you'll get a nicely shaped circular loop rather than an oval.

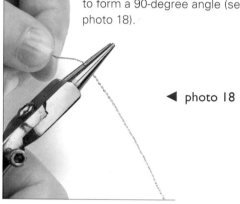

◄ photo 19

3. Coil the loose end of your wire(s) around the vertical stem twice, making the first coil as close to your loop as possible (see photo 20) and working your way down. Finish off the wire(s).

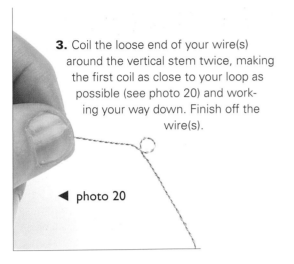

◀ photo 20

hanger-style wire-wrapped loop

1. Insert your wire through the hole of the briolette, leaving about 1 inch (2.5 cm) of wire on one side and the remainder on the other (see photo 21).

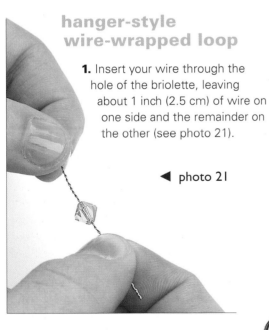

◀ photo 21

2. Cross the two ends above the briolette, making a hanger shape and leaving enough space that the briolette can still swing on the wire (see photo 22).

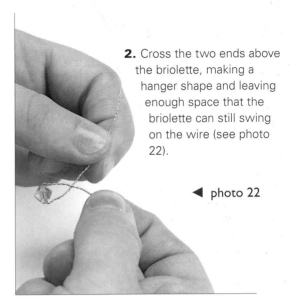

◀ photo 22

3. Coil the short end around the long end once or twice until secure (see photo 23). Clip that tail.

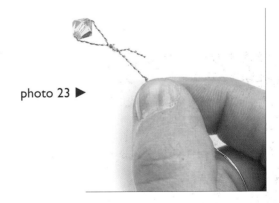

photo 23 ▶

4. Straighten the remaining length of wire, and wire-wrap a loop as explained above.

shaping frames

Some of the more advanced projects in this book call for frames made of less flexible wire to which the twisted wire portions of the piece will later be attached. As mentioned previously, you'll need to treat less flexible wires a little differently than 28-gauge wire.

▶ **If you accidentally get a bend in your wire when forming a round or or oval hoop, you can usually press it out by squeezing that section of the wire with flat-nose pliers at its wider end.**

shaping 20-gauge half-hard wire

Making a frame out of 20-gauge half-hard wire is best done with your fingers—using either type of pliers will cause undesirable little bends in the wire. Depending on the shape you're making, use one of the following techniques.

1. If making a round or oval frame, simply nudge the wire with the fingers of one hand against the forefinger of your other hand, bit by bit along the length of the wire, shaping it very gradually until it looks like the project photo. You may find it easier to use a mandrel or some other round rod or pole to shape the curved section.

2. If you're making a diamond-shaped frame, use your flat-nose pliers to bend the wire against (not with) the curve at its center point. Then bend it, again against the curve, at the other two points called for in the pattern, making sure that you make these two bends equidistant from the bottom center point of the diamond.

shaping memory wire

Memory wire is much more difficult to mold, since it's meant to "remember" its shape. However, it can be bent using flat-nose pliers and, despite its natural resilience, you can curve or uncurve it to a certain extent by applying pressure at regular intervals, and then repeating the process until the curves have been tightened up or loosened up as needed.

curling
a closed loop

All of the frames called for in this book require closed loops at their ends. Follow these steps to curl a closed loop:

1. Grasp the very tip of your 20-gauge or memory wire with your round-nose pliers. Rotating just your wrist (not your arm), curl the wire down until you've reached the comfortable limit of your wrist.

2. Reposition your pliers and continue curling the wire until metal touches metal (loop made).

3. Grasp the other side of your loop and tip the loop back a bit so that it's centered on the end of the wire (this step isn't necessary with frames made of memory wire). You may need to close up the loop a bit after this step.

attaching
filigrees
to frames

You can attach a filigree to a frame in two ways: by making beaded loops of 28-gauge wire around the frame; or by coiling plain 28-gauge wire around it, securing the filigree at key points of contact by bringing the wire through the filigree, pulling the wire tight, and then continuing on with the looping or coiling until the next point of contact is reached. First, however, the filigree should be "tacked" in place in order to gauge its best positioning and to aid you in fine-tuning its shape.

tacking filigrees in place

Use scraps or short pieces of 28-gauge wire to wrap around the frame and the motif or branch of your filigree at each projected point of contact. To do this, simply insert a wire through the filigree (either into a motif or around the curve of a branch), bringing the other end of the wire around the frame and back through the filigree again once or twice as needed to secure it in place. Don't pull the tacking wire too tight, or it will be difficult to remove it once it has served its purpose.

anchoring a new wire
to your frame

Leaving a ½-inch (1.3 cm) tail (this gives you something to hold on to as you get your coil started), wrap your wire tightly several times around the frame at the point specified by the pattern, placing each new coil close up against the previous one.

attaching a filigree to a frame

The framed filigrees in this book are attached either by coiling or by looping on beads.

coiling

Once you've anchored your new wire to the frame, continue wrapping it very tightly, placing each new coil right up against the previous one to create an even, continuous look. Take care not to place one coil on top of another. When a desirable point of contact for your filigree is reached, remove the tacking wire, bring your new wire through the filigree itself (either through a motif or around the curve of a branch) and, pulling the wire tight, continue on with the coiling until the next point of contact is reached.

To a certain extent, you can slide the coils along the frame so that they are pressed more tightly together or spread out a bit. This will bring the points of contact on the filigree closer together or farther apart as needed to make the filigree fit more attractively.

If you're starting the coiling process by covering a closed loop with coils, leave a ½-inch (1.3 cm) tail to give you something to hold on to as you get your coil started. Then, beginning at the unattached end of the loop, coil your 28-gauge wire tightly and neatly around it, feeding the working end of the wire through the loop each time until you've completely covered the loop (the coils will be closer together on the inside of the loop than on the outside). Continue coiling past the closed loop according to your pattern instructions.

looping on beads

Once you've anchored your new wire to the frame, add the number of beads specified by your pattern to your wire. Start wrapping the wire around the frame in the same direction as before, stopping to seat the last bead added on the outer edge of the frame. Hold the bead in place there by pressing it against the frame with one of your fingers, then wrap the wire tightly twice around the frame.

Repeat the steps in the last paragraph (from "add the number of beads . . .") up to the first desirable point of contact for your filigree. Remove the tacking wire, bring your new wire through the filigree itself (either through a motif or around the curve of a branch), and pull the wire tight. Wrap around the frame two times, and then continue looping on beads until the next point of contact is reached.

You'll sometimes find that the first desirable point of contact is located prior to where the first loop of beads would begin. In that case, simply make your first attachment immediately after anchoring your wire to the frame, and then proceed with looping on beads as above.

caring for wire & bead jewelry

The very thin wires used to make twisted wire jewelry give it its special delicate appearance. Unfortunately, these thin wires also make it very flexible, and they can easily be bent out of shape. (Exceptions to this rule include the framed pieces in the more advanced projects, which are relatively sturdy). Avoid damage by taking special care to handle your twisted wire pieces gently and store them properly.

handling your twisted wire jewelry

Use common sense when handling your pieces. Avoid, for example, picking up a twisted wire necklace in one hand and dangling it while making broad gestures. For best results (and an extended life expectancy), pick up pieces flat, supporting their weight evenly on your palms.

Here's some good news: If a piece (or just a branch in a piece) does get bent out of shape, all you have to do is gently nudge it back. Just don't bend it in the same place over and over. Any wire, when bent repeatedly, will eventually become brittle and weak.

storing your twisted wire jewelry

Jewelry made with twisted wire techniques is best stored flat. As with any jewelry made of metal, storing it in (or under) plastic will slow the oxidation process, which can cause metals to dull or discolor. Plastic freezer bags are excellent for this purpose. Just slide the piece inside, squeeze or press the bag down gently to burp out the air, and seal it tightly.

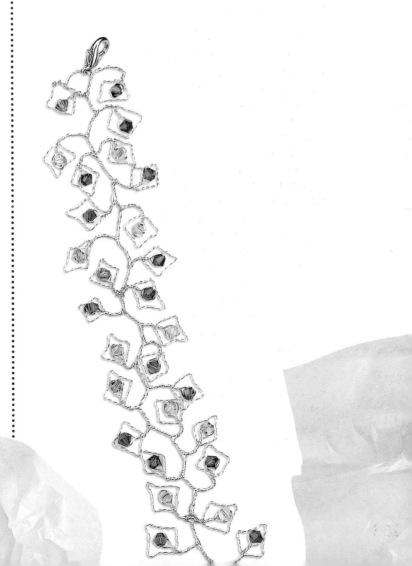

motif boutique

When a project lists the motifs used for that piece, turn back to this section. It's a handy guide to the most common motifs (patterns of twists and beads) you'll be combining to make your bead and wire jewelry.

Many of the motifs are quite similar and vary only in the number of beads used. You'll also find that the same motif can produce a variety of looks, depending on the beads used. As you become more familiar with these motifs, the process of creating jewelry will become easier and easier.

flower motifs

The following flower motifs consist of a number of "petal" beads (usually all the same) formed into a circle or loop with a different bead (usually one that offers some color contrast) positioned in its center.

five-petal flower motif

You can use this motif to begin a piece or you can add it to a work in progress.

beginning a new piece with a five-petal flower motif

1. Add the five "petal" beads called for in the pattern to your wire and slide them down to its center point. (Note: From this point on, the wires on either side of your beads will be referred to as two separate wires.) Form the beads into a loop with the wires crossed at its base (see figure 1). Secure the loop in place by wrapping one of your wires (this will be your working wire) around the other (now your dormant wire) twice very tightly right up against the base of the loop (see figure 2).

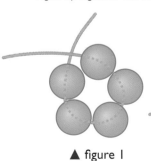

▲ figure 1

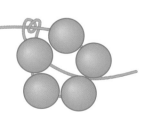

▲ figure 2

2. Bring your working wire all the way under the loop and then back over across the front of it. Add the "center" bead called for in the pattern, and position it in the center of your loop (see figure 3).

▲ figure 3

3. Holding your two wires between the thumb and forefinger of your left hand right up against the base of your loop, give the loop two or three half-twists, just enough to secure it in place.

4. Back your left hand away from this twisted portion bit by bit, still holding your two wires just slightly apart between the thumb and forefinger of your left hand as you twist the motif with your right hand, thus beginning your main stem (see the tips on page 17). Keep twisting until you have the length of main stem called for in the pattern (see figure 4).

▲ figure 4

adding a five-petal flower motif to a work in progress

1. Add the five "petal" beads called for in the pattern to one of your wires (this is now your working wire) and slide them down toward your main stem. Holding them at the called-for distance from the main stem (i.e., "on a ⅜-inch [9.5 mm] branch"), form them into a loop with the wires crossed at the loop's base. Secure the loop in place by wrapping the loose end of your working wire around the part between the motif and your main stem twice very tightly right up against the base of the loop.

2. Bring the working end of your wire all the way under the loop and then over and across the front of it. Add the "center" bead called for in the pattern, and position it in the center of your loop.

3. Holding the two sections of your working wire (the loose end and the section that lies between the motif and your main stem) between the thumb and forefinger of your left hand right up against the base of your loop, give the loop two or three half-twists, just enough to secure it in place.

4. Back your left hand away from the twisted portion bit by bit, still holding your two wires just slightly apart between the thumb and forefinger of your left hand as you twist the motif with your right hand (see the tips on page 17). Continue until the branch is twisted all the way back to the main stem.

six-petal flower motif

To create this motif, begin with the six "petal" beads called for in the pattern, and work as for the Five-Petal Flower Motif.

eight-petal flower motif

Similarly, begin with the eight "petal" beads called for in the pattern, and work as for the Five-Petal Flower Motif.

ten-petal flower motif

You guessed it—begin with the 10 "petal" beads called for in the pattern, and work as for the Five-Petal Flower Motif.

five-petal flower motif with beaded outline

To create this motif variety:

1. Work as for the Five-Petal Flower Motif through step 3.

2. Add to your working wire the number of seed beads called for in the pattern, and bring the wire up from back to front between the next two petals of your motif, pulling the wire tightly, so that it forms an outline around the first bead five times (see figure 5).

3. Work steps 3 to 4 as for the Five-Petal Flower Motif.

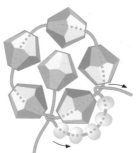

figure 5 ▶

leaf motifs

Leaf motifs consist of one or more beads (all the same or not) formed into a loop. Single-leaf motifs are made from a single loop of wire with beads, while double-branch motifs feature loops of beaded wire at the end of two or more branches.

one-bead single-leaf motif

You can use this motif to begin a piece or you can add it to a work in progress.

beginning a new piece with a one-bead single-leaf motif

1. Add the bead called for in the pattern to your wire, and slide it down to the wire's center point. From this point on, the wires on either side of your bead will be referred to as two separate wires.

2. Holding the two wires between the thumb and forefinger of your left hand right up against the base of your bead, give the loop two or three half-twists, just enough to secure it in place (see figure 6).

▲ figure 6

3. Back your left hand away from the twisted portion bit by bit, still holding your two wires just slightly apart between the thumb and forefinger of your left hand as you twist the motif with your right hand (again, see the tips on page 17). Continue until you have the length of main stem called for in the pattern.

adding a one-bead single-leaf motif to a work in progress

1. Add the bead called for in the pattern to one of your wires (this is now your working wire), and slide it down toward the main stem.

2. Holding it at the called-for distance from the main stem (i.e., "on a ⅜-inch [9.5 mm] branch"), fold the wire back over the bead and, holding the two wires between the thumb and forefinger of your left hand right up against the base of your bead, give the loop two or three half-twists, just enough to secure it in place. This will be similar to the process shown in figure 6, only you will be working on a branch off the main stem.

3. Back your left hand away from the twisted portion bit by bit, still holding your two wires just slightly apart between the thumb and forefinger of your left hand as you twist the motif with your right hand. Continue until the branch is twisted all the way back to the main stem

three-bead single-leaf motif

You can use this motif to begin a piece or you can add it to a work in progress.

beginning a new piece with a three-bead single-leaf motif

1. Add the three beads called for in the pattern to your wire, and slide them down to its center point. (Note: From this point on, the wires on either side of your beads will be referred to as two separate wires.) Form the beads into a loop with the wires crossed at its base.

2. Secure the loop in place by wrapping one of your wires (this will be your working wire) around the other (now your dormant wire) twice very tightly right up against the base of the loop. This will be similar to the process shown in figure 6, only with three beads instead of one.

3. Back your left hand away from this twisted portion bit by bit, still holding your two wires just slightly apart between the thumb and forefinger of your left hand as you twist the motif with your right hand, thus beginning your main stem (see the tips on page 17). Keep twisting until you have the length of main stem called for in the pattern

adding a three-bead single-leaf motif to a work in progress

1. Add the three beads called for in the pattern to one of your wires (this will be your working wire), and slide them down toward the main stem. Holding them at the called-for distance from the main stem (i.e., "on a ⅜-inch [9.5 mm] branch"), form them into a loop with the wires crossed at the loop's base.

2. Secure the loop in place by wrapping the loose end of your working wire around the part between the motif and your main stem twice very tightly right up against the base of the loop.

3. Back your left hand away from the twisted portion bit by bit, still holding your two wires just slightly apart between the thumb and forefinger of your left hand as you twist the motif with your right hand (see the tips on page 17). Continue until the branch is twisted all the way back to the main stem.

five-bead single-leaf motif

Begin with the five beads called for in the pattern, and work as for the Three-Bead Single-Leaf Motif.

seven-bead single leaf motif

Begin with the seven beads called for in the pattern, and work as for the Three-Bead Single-Leaf Motif.

one-bead single-leaf motif with beaded outline

Here are the steps for this motif variety:

1. Work as for the One-Bead Single-Leaf Motif through step 2.

2. Add to your working wire the number of seed beads called for in the pattern, and loop them around the bicone, wrapping the tail twice around the base of the motif to secure the loop in place (see figure 7).

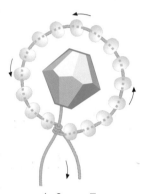

▲ figure 7

3. Shape the loop to fit attractively around the bicone.

4. Finish off as in step 3 for the One-Bead Single-Leaf Motif.

one-bead single-leaf motif with unbeaded outline

This motif can only be worked when using doubled wires. Follow these steps:

1. Using two wires as one, work as for the One-Bead Single-Leaf Motif through step 2.

2. Twist the two pieces of your working wire for a length of about 1 inch (2.5 cm). Using your flat-nose pliers, bend this section at three points so that it forms a diamond shape that outlines the bicone.

3. Work step 3 as for the One-Bead Single-Leaf Motif.

double-branch motif

Basic motifs can literally "branch out" when you include them in Double-Branch Motifs. The examples shown and described here feature Three-Bead Single Leaf Motifs, but you can place different single-leaf motifs at the ends of your branches, depending on your design.

main branch with one sub-branch

1. Make your first motif as for the Three-Bead Single-Leaf Motif through step 2.

2. Back your left hand away from the twisted portion bit by bit, still holding your two wires just slightly apart between the thumb and forefinger of your left hand as you twist the motif with your right hand (see the tips on page 17). Stop when the branch is twisted halfway back to the main stem. This is your "main branch."

3. Add the beads for the second motif called for in the pattern to your working wire, and slide them down toward the "main branch." Holding them at the called-for distance from the "main branch" (i.e., "on a ⅜-inch [9.5 mm] branch"), form them into a loop with the wires crossed at the loop's base. Secure the new motif in place as before.

4. Continue twisting as above until this new "sub-branch" is twisted all the way back to your "main branch."

5. Twist your "main branch" all the way back to your main stem.

main branch with two sub-branches

1. Make your first motif as for the Three-Bead Single-Leaf Motif through step 2.

2. Back your left hand away from the twisted portion bit by bit, still holding your two wires just slightly apart between the thumb and forefinger of your left hand as you twist the motif with your right hand (see the tips on page 17). Stop when the branch is twisted one third of the way back to the main stem. This is your "main branch."

3. Add the beads for the second motif called for in the pattern to your working wire, and slide them down toward the "main branch." Holding them at the called-for distance from the "main branch" (i.e., "on a ⅜-inch [9.5 mm] branch"), form them into a loop with the wires crossed at the loop's base. Secure the new motif in place as before.

4. Continue twisting as above until this new "sub-branch" is twisted all the way back to your "main branch."

5. Twist your "main branch" another one third of the way back to your main stem.

6. Repeat steps 3 and 4.

7. Twist your "main branch" all the way back to your main stem.

triple-prong candelabra motif

This motif consists of repeating three identical motifs in a row with no twisted section of main stem in between them. The first is made on a long branch, the second on a medium branch, and the third on a short branch.

1. Work the first of your three motifs on a 1½-inch (3.8 cm) branch as for the Three-Bead Single-Leaf Motif, and twist back to your main stem.

2. Without twisting a section of main stem, work your second motif on a 1-inch (2.5 cm) branch.

3. Without twisting a section of main stem, work your third motif on a ½-inch (1.3 cm) branch.

4. If there is any space between the base of your Triple-Prong Candelabra Motif and your main stem, hold your working wire at the main stem between the thumb and forefinger of your left hand, and twist the entire triple motif with your right to close up the gap.

cocktail hour
necklace & earrings

Day or night, you'll be a temptress with this black-and-silver necklace and earrings set.

necklace

▶ what you need

- Basic Tool Kit (see page 10)
- 3 yards (2.74 m) of 28-gauge black craft wire
- 25 black 3 x 5 or 4 x 6 mm briolettes
- 40 to 45 metallic silver and hematite gray 3 mm fire-polished beads
- 1 gram of silver-lined crystal size 11° seed beads
- 52 to 56 crystal AB bugle beads
- 3 grams of black opaque size 11° seed beads
- 6 to 12 black 3 mm fire-polished beads
- Black spring-lock or lobster-claw clasp
- 6 mm soldered ring or extender chain

▶ motifs

- Five-Petal Flower, page 30
- Five-Bead Single Leaf, page 33
- Triple-Prong Candelabra, page 35

▶ step by step

1 Cut a 2-foot (61 cm) piece of wire.

2 Using briolettes for the petals and a silver fire-polished bead (FP) for the center, begin with a Five-Petal Flower Motif. This will be the front-center point of your necklace. Twist a ⅜-inch (9.5 mm) section of main stem.

▶ **After step 1, and throughout the remainder of the floral portion of this necklace, you will be switching from one side of the main stem to the other side for each new motif.**

3 Using three gray and/or silver FP with single silver-lined seed beads between them, make a Five-Bead Single-Leaf Motif on a ⅜-inch (9.5 mm) branch. Twist a ⅜-inch (9.5 mm) section of main stem.

4 Repeat step 3.

5 Using three pairs of bugle beads with single black seed beads between them, make a Triple-Prong Candelabra Motif. Twist a ⅜-inch (9.5 mm) section of main stem.

DIMENSIONS: 18 inches (45.7 cm) long

6 Repeat step 5.

7 Using briolettes for the petals and a silver FP for the center, make a Five-Petal Flower Motif on a ⅜-inch (9.5 mm) branch. Twist a ⅜-inch (9.5 mm) section of main stem.

8 Repeat steps 3 through 7.

9 Finish off as explained in the Basics section on page 21.

10 Return to the initial Five-Petal Flower Motif and add another 2-foot (61 cm) piece of wire as explained in the Basics section on page 18. Twist a ⅜-inch (9.5 mm) section of main stem.

11 Repeat steps 2 through 9. The center floral section is now completed.

12 Using round-nose pliers, tweak the strip of filigree by gently curving the branches of the motifs toward the center point. If you want a less formal, more free-form look, try twisting the branches in different directions.

13 Cut the remainder of the wire in four pieces.

14 Join one piece of wire at its center point to one end of the floral filigree strip as explained in the Basics section on page 18. Add a second wire at the same spot. You should now have four wires to work with.

15 Position a FP or bugle bead on any of the wires an inch (2.5 cm) or two from where you joined them. Bring the end of the wire back around and through the bead again from the same direction as before, making a loop around one side of the bead. Holding the bead firmly in place, pull the tail of the wire until the loop snugs up tightly around the side of the bead.

16 Repeat step 13 several times at random intervals along the same wire, stopping about 2 inches (5 cm) short of your desired length for the necklace.

17 Repeat steps 13 and 14 for each of the remaining three wires, staggering the beads to give them a random effect.

18 Measuring first for the desired length of this side of the necklace, thread all four wires through the loop on the clasp and double the wires back. Holding all the wires between the thumb and forefinger of one hand, twist the clasp with the other, four to six times as needed for security, making sure that the tails end up on the front side of the necklace. Clip the tails.

19 Repeat steps 14 through 18 for the other side of the necklace.

20 Shape the necklace so that it curves nicely around the neck.

earrings

▶ what you need

- Basic Tool Kit (see page 10)
- 1 foot (30.5 cm) of 28-gauge black craft wire
- 6 black 3 x 5 or 4 x 6 mm briolettes
- 6 crystal AB bugle beads
- 6 black opaque size 11° seed beads
- 1 metallic silver or hematite gray 3 mm fire-polished bead
- Pair of black base-metal ear wires

▶ motifs

- One-Bead Single Leaf, page 32
- Three-Bead Single Leaf, page 33

▶ step by step

1 Cut a 10-inch (25.4 cm) piece of wire.

2 Using a briolette, begin with a One-Bead Single-Leaf Motif. Twist a ⅛-inch (3 mm) section of main stem.

▶ **From this point on, all motifs except the last will be on the same side of the main stem.**

3 Using a briolette, make another One-Bead Single-Leaf Motif. Twist a ⅛-inch (3 mm) section of main stem.

4 Repeat step 3.

5 Using two bugle beads with a black seed bead between them, make a Three-Bead Single-Leaf Motif. Twist a ⅛-inch (3 mm) section of main stem.

6 Repeat step 5 twice.

7 Using a gray or silver FP, make a One-Bead Single-Leaf Motif on a ⅛-inch (3 mm) branch on the opposite side of the main stem. Twist a 1-inch (2.5 cm) section of main stem.

8 Attach the ear wire as explained in the Basics section on page 24.

9 Make a second earring exactly like the first, and simply turn it over before attaching it to the ear wire to get a mirror image of the first.

10 Using round-nose pliers, tweak the filigrees by gently curving the branches of the motifs all in the same direction or, for a less formal look, in different directions.

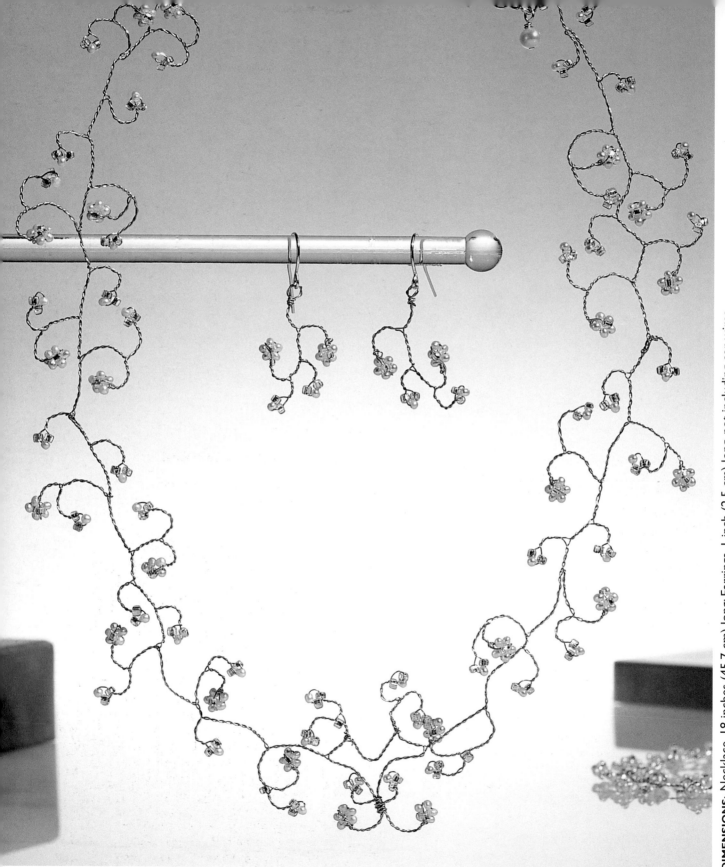

DIMENSIONS: Necklace, 18 inches (45.7 cm) long; Earrings, 1 inch (2.5 cm) long, not including ear wires

fancy
wedding set

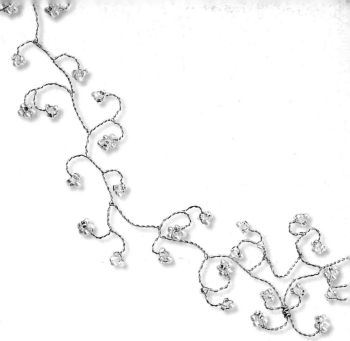

Glittering beads and wire tendrils enfold you in this four-piece set, a fine choice for a special occasion.

necklace

▶ what you need

- **Basic Tool Kit** (see page 10)
- 13 feet (3.9 m) of 28-gauge craft wire or dead-soft sterling silver wire
- 180 pearls, 2 mm
- 8 grams of silver-lined size 11° crystal seed beads
- Lobster-claw clasp
- 1 soldered ring or extender chain, 6 mm
- 1 pearl, 4 mm
- Silver head pin

▶ motifs

- Double-Branch, page 34
- Five-Petal Flower, page 30
- Three-Bead Single Leaf, page 33

▶ step by step

1 Cut a 3-foot (.91 m) piece of wire.

▶ **You will need to add more wire as necessary (see page 18).**

All Five-Petal Flower Motifs in this pattern will consist of pearls for the petals and a seed bead for the center. All Three-Bead Single Leaf Motifs in this pattern will contain two seed beads with one pearl between them on a ⅜-inch (9.5 mm) branch. All Double-Branch Motifs will consist of a Five-Petal Flower Motif worked on a ¾-inch (1.9 cm) main branch with a Three-Bead Single-Leaf Motif on a ⅜-inch (9.5 mm) side branch beginning about a third of the way back toward the main stem.

2 Begin with a Five-Petal Flower Motif. This will be one side of the front center point of the necklace.

▶ **Twist a ⅜- to ½-inch (9.5 mm to 1.3 cm) section of main stem between each motif.**

3 Make a Three-Bead Single-Leaf Motif on the left side of the main stem.

4 On the opposite side of the main stem, work a Double-Branch Motif.

5 Repeat step 4.

6 On the same side of the main stem, repeat step 3.

7 Repeat step 4 twice.

8 Repeat step 3 twice on the opposite side of the main stem.

9 Repeat steps 7 and 8.

10 Repeat step 4 twice.

11 Repeat step 3 on the opposite side of the main stem.

12 Repeat steps 7 through 9, measuring the length of the strip after every motif or two. Stop when you have reached 7 inches (17.8 cm), or 1 inch (2.5 cm) short of the desired length for this half of the necklace.

13 Repeat step 4 as needed until desired length is reached.

14 Twist a 1-inch (2.5 cm) section of main stem.

15 Repeat steps 1 through 14 for the other side of the necklace, making the first Three-Bead Single-Leaf Motif on the right-hand side of the main stem instead of the left.

16 Tweak and shape both sides of the necklace as shown in the photograph. If you want a less formal, more free-form look, try twisting the branches in random directions.

17 Cut a 2-inch (5 cm) piece of wire. Lay the two sides of the necklace out with the center ends touching, as shown in the photograph. Coil the wire around both main stems just below the first Three-Bead Single-Leaf Motif branch (as shown in figure 1). Make a few more coils just above the motif. Finish off, as explained in the Basics section on page 21.

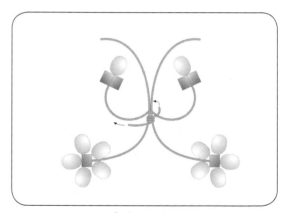

▲ figure 1

18 Cut two 3-inch (7.6 cm) pieces of wire. Holding the two wires just slightly apart, twist a ½-inch (1.3 cm) section at their center point (double wire addition begun).

19 Working at one end of this double-wire addition, coil the tails around the lower end of one of your first Double-Branch Motifs (see figure 2). End at the front side of the necklace, and clip the tails.

20 Working at the other end of this double-wire addition, repeat step 19, coiling the tails around the lower end of the Double-Branch Motif on the other side of the necklace (see figure 2 again).

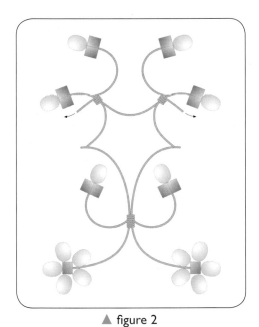

▲ figure 2

21 Add the clasp and extender chain as explained in the Basics section on page 24.

22 Using the head pin, wire-wrap the 4 mm pearl to the bottom link of the extender chain.

23 Shape the necklace so that it curves nicely around the neck. Tweak some more if needed.

bracelet

▶ what you need

- BasicTool Kit (see page 10)
- 6 feet (1.83 m) of 28-gauge silver craft wire or dead-soft sterling silver wire
- 120 pearls, 2mm
- 2 grams of silver-lined size 11° crystal seed beads
- Lobster-claw clasp
- Soldered ring, 6 mm

▶ motifs

- Five-Petal Flower, page 30
- Three-Bead Single Leaf, page 33

▶ step by step

1 Cut a 3-foot (.91 m) piece of wire. You will need to add more wire as necessary (see page 18).

2 Insert the wire into the loop on your clasp and twist the clasp to make a ¼-inch (6 mm) section of main stem.

3 Using pearls for the petals and a seed bead for the center, make a Five-Petal Flower Motif on a ⅛-inch (3 mm) branch. Twist a ¼-inch (6 mm) section of main stem.

4 Repeat step 3 on the opposite side of the main stem.

5 Using two seed beads with one 2 mm pearl between them, make a Three-Bead Single Leaf Motif on a ⅛-inch (3 mm) branch on the opposite side of the main stem. Twist a ¼-inch (6 mm) section of main stem.

6 Repeat step 5.

7 Repeat steps 3 through 6 until you reached the desired total length of your bracelet, minus ½ inch (1.3 cm). For example, the pictured bracelet is 7½ inches (19.1 cm) overall, with the motifs stopping at 7 inches (17.8 cm).

8 Insert both wires through the soldered ring, and twist the ring four or five times. Finish off as explained in the Basics section on page 21.

earrings

▶ what you need

- **Basic Tool Kit** (see page 10)
- 2 feet (61 cm) of 28-gauge silver craft wire or dead-soft sterling silver wire
- 24 white 2 mm pearls
- 1 gram of silver-lined size 11° crystal seed beads
- Pair of silver ear wires

▶ motifs

- Five-Petal Flower, page 30
- Three-Bead Single Leaf, page 33

▶ step by step

1 Cut the wire in half.

2 Using pearls for the petals and a seed bead for the center, make a Five-Petal Flower Motif. Twist a ¼-inch (6 mm) section of main stem.

3 Using two seed beads with one pearl between them, make a Three-Bead Single-Leaf Motif on a ¼-inch (6mm) branch. Twist a ⅜-inch (9.5 mm) section of main stem.

4 Repeat step 3 on the same side of the main stem.

5 On the same side of the main stem, make another Five-Petal Flower Motif on a ⅜-inch (9.5 mm) branch. Twist a 1-inch (2.5 cm) section of main stem.

6 Wire-wrap a loop, and cut the tails.

7 Repeat steps 2 through 6 for the other earring, making it as similar to the first as possible. Flip the flowers over to get a mirror image, if desired.

8 Attach ear wires to the top loops, as explained in the Basics section on page 24.

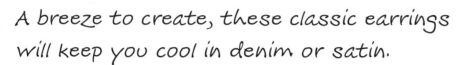

blue note
earrings

A breeze to create, these classic earrings will keep you cool in denim or satin.

▶ what you need

- **Basic Tool Kit** (see page 10)
- 3 feet (.91 m) of 28-gauge craft wire or dead-soft sterling silver wire
- 2 blue 3 x 5 or 4 x 6 mm briolettes
- 12 blue 4-mm crystal bicone beads
- Pair of ear wires

▶ motifs

- One-Bead Single Leaf, page 32

▶ step by step

1 Cut four 9-inch (22.9 cm) pieces of wire.

2 Insert two pieces up to their center points through a briolette. Give all four wires three half-twists, making sure to leave enough space between the top of the briolette and the point where you begin twisting so the briolette can move freely. The first section of the main stem is now made.

3 Separate the four wires. Using only one wire, make a One-Bead Single Leaf on the shortest possible branch (just enough to secure the bicone in place) on one side of the main stem.

▶ **The best way to limit the length of the branch is to leave very little length for twisting, and then grip the wires between your thumb and forefinger at the bottom of the motif before giving no more than two or three half-twists.**

4 Twist a ½-inch (1.3 cm) length of stem, using only the branch wire and one other. The side stem is now made.

5 Repeat steps 3 and 4 on the opposite side of the main stem, using the other two wires.

6 Bring the two side stems together and give them three half-twists. This completes the second section of the main stem.

7 Repeat steps 3 through 6. This completes the third section.

8 Repeat step 3.

9 Give all four wires three half-twists.

10 Wire-wrap a loop with two of the wires, finishing by tightly coiling the two several times around all four of the wires of the main stem. Clip all tails and attach them to an ear wire by opening the loop on the ear wire, adding the earring, and closing the loop securely.

11 Tweak the earrings by opening up marquise-shaped spaces between the side stems and by turning all the crystals as needed to face front.

12 Repeat steps 2 through 11 for the second earring.

DIMENSIONS: 2 inches (5 cm) long, not including ear wires

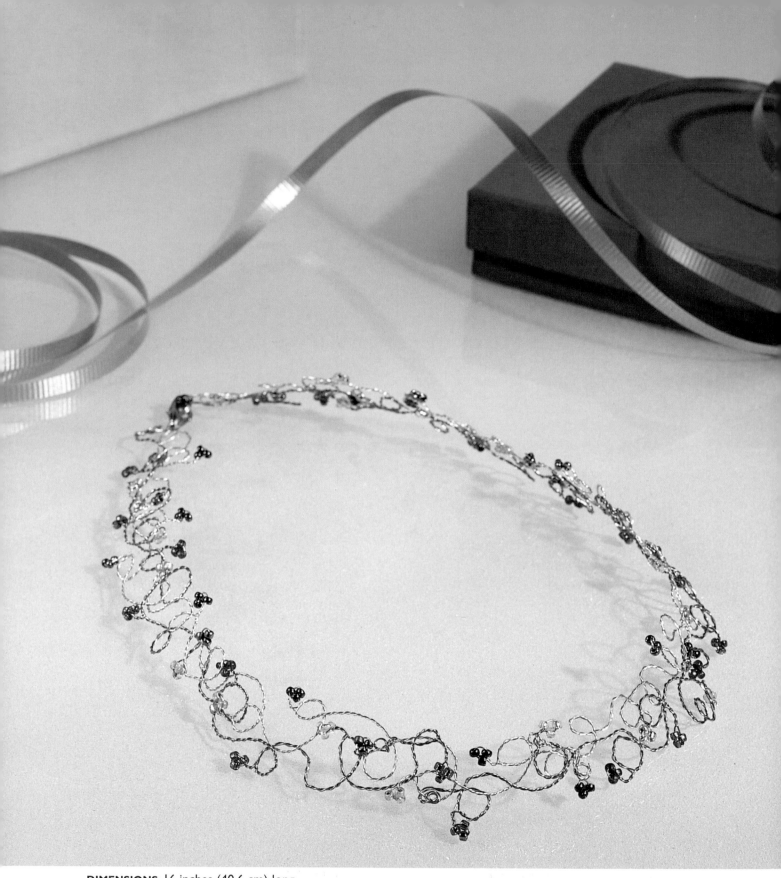

DIMENSIONS: 16 inches (40.6 cm) long

gold & bronze
twining vines necklace

High fashion goes au naturale with spontaneous wire swirls and golden beads.

▶ what you need

- Basic Tool Kit (see page 10)
- 10 feet (3.2 m) each of gold and natural (or copper) 28-gauge craft wire
- 3 grams each, size 11° seed beads:
  - Crystal gold-lined
  - Transparent or lined amber
  - Transparent or lined russet
  - Metallic bronze
  - Metallic brown
- Lobster claw clasp
- 6 mm soldered ring or extender chain

▶ motif

Three-Bead Single Leaf, page 33

▶ step by step

1 Cut a 3-foot (.91 m) piece of gold wire.

2 Begin with a Three-Bead Single-Leaf Motif in any one color on a ¼-inch (6 mm) branch. Twist a 1½-inch (3.8 cm) section of main stem.

3 Make a Three-Bead Single-Leaf Motif on a ¼-inch (6 mm) branch on either side of the main stem. Twist a 1½-inch (3.8 cm) section of main stem.

▶ **You can rotate the colors as you go, or choose them randomly.**

4 Repeat step 3 on the opposite side of the main stem 23 times, adding wire as needed (see the section Adding New Wire on page 18).

5 Tweak and shape the filigree strip as shown in the photograph.

▶ **The tweaking on this piece is extensive and involves making loops and convoluted curves in the main stems. Just keep tweaking and shaping until the filigree strip is 15 inches (38.1 cm), or the desired total length, minus 1 inch (2.5 cm) for the clasp. If the strip doesn't look convoluted enough, repeat step 4 a few times to add length and then re-tweak to shorten it again, while making the strip more dense and complex.**

6 Repeat steps 1 through 5 using natural wire.

7 Interlace the two strips of filigree by crossing and re-crossing them over and around each other, gently pulling the motifs of each strip around in front of or behind the stems and branches of the other until the two strips are securely joined. Tweak and shape some more as needed.

8 Attach the clasp and ring, as explained on page 24, inserting all four tails before twisting.

DIMENSIONS: 15½ inches (39.4 cm) long

spring garden
quartet

Bright colors abound in this necklace,
bracelet, earrings, and tiara set.

necklace

▶ what you need

- **Basic Tool Kit** (see page 10)
- 2½ yards (2.29 m) of 28-gauge craft wire or dead-soft sterling silver wire
- 4 mm crystal AB bicone beads:
  - 11 pink
  - 16 blue
  - 16 purple
  - 11 yellow
  - 18 green
- Spring lock or lobster claw clasp
- 6 mm soldered ring or extender chain

▶ color key

Color A = pink
Color B = blue
Color C = purple
Color D = yellow
Color E = green

▶ motifs for all pieces

- Five-Petal Flower, page 30
- One-Bead Single Leaf, page 32

▶ step by step

1 Cut the wire in half and set one piece aside.

2 Using Color A crystals for the petals and one Color D crystal for the center, begin with a Five-Petal Flower Motif. This will be the front center point of the necklace. Twist a ⅜-inch (9.5 mm) main stem.

3 Divide the number of crystals in half, setting aside one group for later use.

4 Using a Color E crystal, make a One-Bead Single-Leaf Motif on a ⅜-inch (9.5 mm) branch on one side of the main stem. Twist a ⅜-inch (9.5 mm) section of main stem.

5 Repeat step 4 on the other side of the main stem.

6 Using Color B crystals for the petals and one Color D crystal for the center, make a Five-Petal Flower Motif (see page 30) on a ⅜-inch (9.5 mm)

DIMENSIONS: Approx. 1 inch (2.5 cm) high

tiara

▶ what you need

- Basic Tool Kit (see page 10)
- 3 yards (2.7 m) of 28-gauge craft wire or dead-soft sterling silver wire
- ¼ to ⅜-inch (6 to 9.5 mm) wide, plain, flat metal or plastic headband
- 100 blue 4 mm fire-polished glass beads
- 4 mm crystal AB bicone beads:
    - 10 pink
    - 10 blue
    - 10 purple
    - 6 yellow
    - 10 green

▶ step by step

1 Cut a 1-yard (.91 m) piece of wire, and wrap one end of it tightly around the headband several times, about an inch (2.5 cm) from one end, to anchor it in place.

2 Add one 4 mm fire-polished bead to the wire and, positioning the bead at the front side of the headband, wrap the wire tightly around the headband twice to anchor the bead in place.

3 Repeat step 2, adding wire as necessary, as explained in the Basics section on page 18, until you have reached a point about an inch (2.5 cm) from the other end of the headband. Finish off by wrapping the wire an extra time or two around the frame.

4 Cut a piece of wire about 16 inches (40.6 cm) long. Find the center point at the front of the headband, and join one end of the new wire there by wrapping it tightly around, between two of the fire-polished beads three times.

5 Using Color A crystals for the petals and one Color D crystal for the center, make a Five Petal Flower on a ¾-inch (1.9 cm) branch.

6 Twist the branch all the way down to the headband, and wrap the wire around the headband once in the same spot where you began. Wrap the wire around the headband one bead over, and then again one bead over from that.

7 Using one Color E crystal, make a One-Bead Single-Leaf Motif on a ¼-inch (6 mm) branch.

8 Repeat step 6.

9 Using Color C crystals for the petals, repeat step 5 on a ⅝-inch (1.6 cm) branch. Repeat step 6.

10 Repeat step 7 and then repeat step 6.

11 Using Color B crystals for the petals, repeat step 5 on a ½-inch (1.3 cm) branch. Repeat step 6.

12 Repeat 7 and then repeat step 6 three times.

13 Wrap wire firmly around the headband three times, and clip tail at the front of the headband.

14 Repeat steps 4 through 13, working in the opposite direction from the center point.

15 Twist the branch portions of the two center flowers together. Using round-nose pliers, tweak the strip of filigree by gently curving the branches.

DIMENSIONS: 2¼ inches (5.7 cm) long and 1½ inches (3.8 cm) wide

the arch, and pull until the bead is snugly seated against the arch.

15 Repeat step 14 twice more. Carry the dormant wire across behind the small beads to rejoin the working wire.

16 Repeat steps 13 to 15 eight times more.

17 Repeat step 13. Finish off in the frame loop above the off-white coils.

18 Using the remaining piece of copper wire, attach one end around the frame in the space under the first set of arches, as close to the top of the pendant as possible.

19 Adding five charlottes at a time, loop around the inside edge of the frame (see Looping on Beads on page 28), placing the coils just after the off-white and green coils, until you reach the bottom center point of the frame, and placing the coils just prior to the off-white and green coils as you work up the other side. Finish off just before the last green coils.

20 Press gently against the sides of the frame until its two top closed loops are only ¼ inch (6 mm) or so apart at their nearest point.

21 Using the remaining copper wire, string one 2 mm bead or seed bead and pull it down to the center point on the wire. Thread the wire from front to back through the two frame loops.

22 Bring the tail on one side around and through its frame loop from front to back again twice. Repeat for the other side, pulling it tight enough that the two frame loops are separated only by the small bead's width.

23 To make the piece into a pin, thread one tail through the remaining 4 mm bead from one side, and the other tail through it from the other side, pulling both tails until the bead is seated evenly across the top of the pin. Finish off each tail by coiling it back around and through the unoccupied section of its frame loop at least twice and then clipping it.

24 Shape the cabochon setting as needed for fit and attractiveness, making sure that it is narrow enough to leave enough gluing surface around the cabochon's back edges. Spread glue liberally around the outer edges of the cab up to the point where it will have no copper-looped beads behind it near the top. Press onto the cameo setting, weighting it down if necessary to hold it firmly in place until the glue has a chance to partially set (about two hours). Let dry for 48 hours before adding the necklace portion. You can also make this pendant into a pin by gluing on a pin back after the pendant has dried.

25 String half of the 4 x 6 beads, adding two copper size 11° seed beads with one off-white size 11° seed bead between them after every fifth bead. Add four copper seed beads, and bring the wire up through the top loop of the bezel between the green wire and the frame. Add seven more seed beads (or the number needed to cover the wire all the way to the same point on the other side of the bezel), alternating between copper and off-white. Bring the wire down through the top loop of the bezel. Add four copper seed beads, and resume the stringing pattern until you have used up all of the 4 x 6 mm beads.

26 Use the crimp beads to add the clasp, as explained in the Basics section on page 24.

8 Repeat steps 6 and 7 twice more.

9 Add a rondelle, and pull it down to (but not over) the twisted section. Twist a ¾-inch (1.9 cm) length of main stem.

10 Add five seed beads, a rondelle, and five more seed beads, and form them into a loop, twisting the wires at the point where they meet (just above the loop) two or three times to secure the loop. Twist a ¾-inch (1.9 cm) length of main stem.

11 Repeat steps 9 and 10 three more times.

12 To make the "bow" shapes, tweak the first half of the necklace by forming the twisted wire section on either side of each beaded loop into a loop, using round-nose pliers to form the loops and making the twisted wire loops large enough to take up all the space between the beaded loops and the single beads between them (see figure 2). In other words, the wire loops will be larger where the twisted section is longer and smaller where the twisted section is shorter. This will give you a graduated necklace.

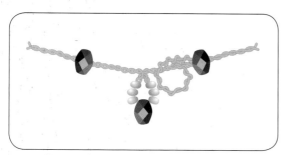

▲ figure 2

13 Measure the necklace at this point. If it is not half as long as you want the finished piece to be minus ¼ inch (6 mm), repeat steps 9 and 10 as needed until it is.

▶ **From this point on, handle the necklace gently so that the loops remain undisturbed. If they do get closed up, you will be able to reshape them later.**

14 Repeat step 9.

15 Add five seed beads, a 3 mm FP, a 4 mm FP, a rondelle, the 6 mm bicone, a rondelle, a 4 mm FP, a 3 mm FP, and five seed beads. Form them into a loop, twisting the wires at the point where they meet (just above the loop) two or three times to secure the loop. Twist a ¾-inch (1.9 cm) length of main stem.

16 Repeat steps 9 and 10 four times (or more if you added extra repeats on the first side for length).

17 Repeat steps 6 and 7 three times.

18 Repeat steps 3 and 4 ten times.

19 Repeat step 3.

20 Add a soldered ring, and finish off as explained in the Basics section on page 21.

earrings

▶ what you need

- Basic Tool Kit (see page 10)
- 3 feet (.91 m) of 28-gauge silver craft wire or dead-soft sterling silver wire
- 1 gram of size 15° silver seed beads or charlottes
- 42 black 3 mm fire-polished beads
- 4 black 4 mm fire-polished beads
- 4 black 3 x 5 mm rondelle beads
- 2 black 6 mm crystal bicones
- Pair of silver ear wires

▶ step by step

1 Cut two 9-inch (22.9 cm) pieces of wire.

2 Holding them just slightly apart, and leaving a 2-inch (5 cm) tail, twist a ¾-inch (1.9 cm) length of main stem at one end (no motif).

3 Add five seed beads, a 3 mm FP, a 4 mm FP, a rondelle, the 6 mm bicone, a rondelle, a 4 mm FP, a 3 mm FP, and five seed beads. Form them into

a loop, twisting the wires at the point where they meet (just above the loop) two or three times to secure the loop. Twist a ¾-inch (1.9 cm) length of main stem.

4 To make the "bow" shape, tweak the earring by forming the twisted wire section on either side of the beaded loop into a loop, using round-nose pliers to form the loops, and making the twisted wire loops large enough to use up the entire twisted length.

5 Bring the two pairs of untwisted wire together and, using them as one wire, wire-wrap a loop at the top of the earring.

6 Add the ear wire as explained in the Basics section on page 24.

7 Repeat steps 1 through 6 for the other earring.

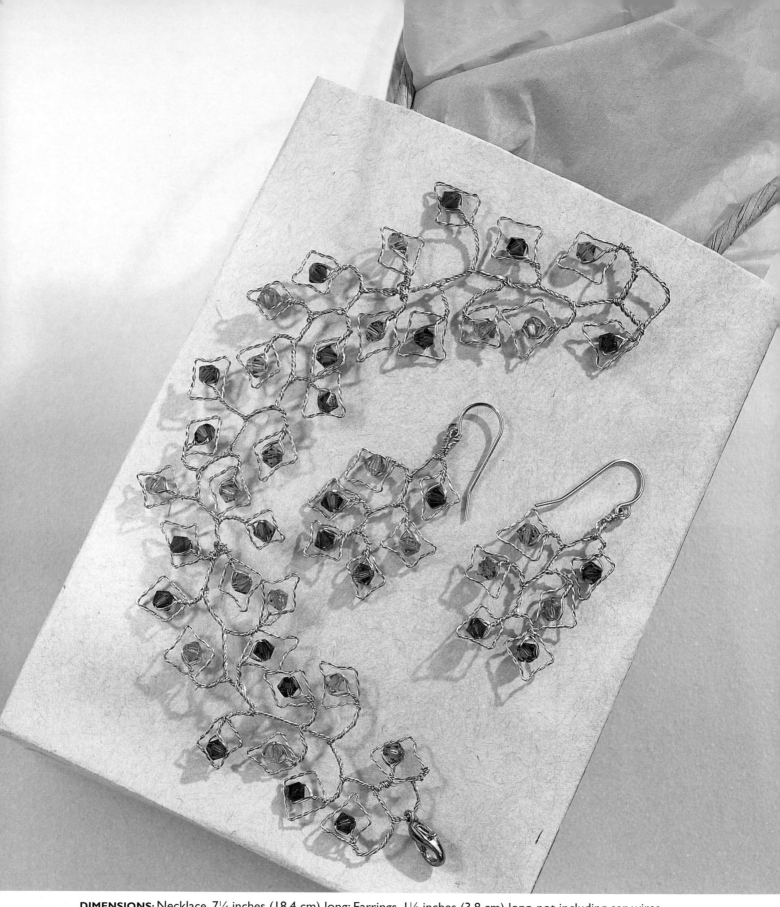

DIMENSIONS: Necklace, 7¼ inches (18.4 cm) long; Earrings, 1½ inches (3.8 cm) long, not including ear wires

autumn leaves
bracelet & earrings

This divine bracelet and earring set borrows the fabulous colors of fall for its inspiration.

bracelet

▶ what you need

- **Basic Tool Kit** (see page 10)
- Chain-nose pliers
- 12 feet (3.7 m) of 28-gauge gold craft wire or dead-soft wire
- 5 to 6 each, 4 mm bicone crystals:
  - Dark brown
  - Amber
  - Burnt orange
  - Orange
  - Red
  - Pale olive or yellow
- Gold lobster claw clasp

▶ motif for both pieces

- One-Bead Single Leaf with Unbeaded Outline, page 34

▶ step by step

1 Cut the wire into two equal pieces. Holding the two wires together with their ends lined up, fold them over at their center point (you now have four wires to work with) and twist into a thick, 1-inch (2.5 cm) section of main stem (no motif).

▶ **From this point on, you will be using two pieces of wire as one on the branches and all four pieces of wire as two on the main stems. Rotate the colors.**

2 Make a One-Bead Single-Leaf Motif with Unbeaded Outline on a ⅜-inch (9.5 mm) branch, twisting back toward the main stem only far enough to secure the motif in place, just three or four half-twists.

3 Twist the two pieces of the working wire for a length of about 1 inch (2.5 cm). Using flat-nose pliers, bend this section at three points so that it forms a diamond shape that outlines the bicone. Holding the working wire against the bottom section of the branch, twist everything back to the main stem.

4 Twist a ¼- to ⅜-inch (6 to 9.5 mm) section of main stem.

5 Repeat steps 2 through 4 on alternating sides of the stem to the desired length minus ½ inch (1.3 cm). Twist an additional ½-inch (1.3 cm) section of main stem.

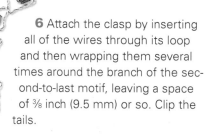

6 Attach the clasp by inserting all of the wires through its loop and then wrapping them several times around the branch of the second-to-last motif, leaving a space of ⅜ inch (9.5 mm) or so. Clip the tails.

7 Wrap the wires at the beginning end of the bracelet several times around the branch of the second motif you made, creating a loop large enough to serve as the other end of the clasp. Clip the tails.

earrings

▶ what you need

- Basic Tool Kit (see page 10)
- Flat-nose pliers
- 6 feet (1.83 m) of 28-gauge gold craft wire or dead-soft wire
- 2 each, 4 mm crystal bicone beads:
  - Dark brown
  - Amber
  - Burnt orange
  - Orange
  - Red
  - Pale olive or yellow
- Pair of gold ear wires

▶ step by step

1 Cut the wire into four equal pieces.

2 Holding two of the wires together with their ends lined up, fold them over at their center point (you now have four wires to work with). Leaving a small loop at the end (to which you will later attach the ear wire), twist all four pieces into a thick, ¼-inch (6 mm) section of main stem (no motif).

▶ **From this point on, you will be using two pieces of wire as one on the branches and all four pieces of wire as two on the main stems. Use one bead of each color.**

3 Make a One-Bead Single-Leaf Motif with Unbeaded Outline on a ¼-inch (6 mm) branch, twisting back toward the main stem only far enough to secure the motif in place, just three or four half-twists.

4 Twist the two pieces of the working wire for a length of about 1 inch (2.5 cm). Using flat-nose pliers, bend this section at three points so that it forms a diamond shape that outlines the bicone. Holding the working wire against the bottom section of the branch, twist everything back to the main stem.

5 Twist a ¼-inch (6 mm) section of main stem.

6 Repeat steps 2 through 5 on alternating sides of the stem five more times. Finish by wrapping the tails around the main stem just far enough to be secure. Clip the tails.

7 Attach the ear wire to the top loop.

8 Repeat steps 2 through 7 for the other earring.

sand & sky
turquoise bracelet

This crystal mosaic bracelet combines vibrant tones of turquoise and amber with delicate wire work.

DIMENSIONS: 8 inches (20.3 cm) long

▶ what you need

- **Basic Tool Kit** (see page 10)
- 12 feet (3.7 m) of turquoise 28-gauge craft wire
- 3 mm fire-polished beads:
    - 20 metallic bronze
    - 20 turquoise
    - 30 dark amber
- 4 mm fire-polished beads:
    - 1 green
    - 20 light amber
- 20 feet (6.1 m) of bronze 28-gauge craft wire
- Toggle clasp

▶ motif

- One-Bead Single Leaf, page 32
- Six-Petal Flower, page 32

▶ step by step

1 Cut a 2-foot (61 cm) piece of turquoise wire.

2 Using metallic bronze for the petals and green for the center, begin with a Six-Petal Flower Motif near one end of the wire.

3 Add a turquoise bead to the long wire, and bring the wire up between the next two petals, pulling it tightly until the bead is secured in place. Repeat six times.

4 Bring the wire up through the next loop of wire, just prior to the turquoise bead holding it. Add a light amber bead, and bring the wire up through the next loop of wire, pulling it firmly but not too tightly until the bead is secured in place. Repeat six times.

5 Bring the wire up through the next loop of wire, just prior to the light amber bead holding it. Add three dark amber beads, and bring the wire up through the next loop, pulling it firmly but not too tightly until the beads are secured in place. Repeat six times. This completes the center flower. Fasten off.

6 Cut the bronze wire into four 5-foot (1.5 m) pieces. Cut the remaining turquoise wire in half. Fold one piece of turquoise wire over at its center point, and twist a 1½-inch (3.8 cm) section of main stem (no motif).

7 Rotating the bead colors, make a One-Bead Single-Leaf Motif on a ½-inch (1.3 cm) branch on one side of the main stem. Twist a 1½-inch (3.8 cm) section of main stem.

8 Repeat step 7 until you run out of wire, ending with a 1-inch (2.5 cm) twisted section of main stem.

9 Repeat step 7 and 8 for the other three pieces of wire.

▶ **The tweaking on this piece is extensive, and involves making loops and convoluted curves in the main stems.**

10 Tweak the filigree strips, making loops and tight curves as necessary until all the strips measure about 3½ inches (8.9 cm) or desired length minus 1½ inches (3.8 cm), not counting the final 1-inch (2.5 cm) main stem section. Don't worry too much about length at this time; just get it fairly close. Exact sizing will be done later.

11 Attach a turquoise strip to the center flower by wrapping its beginning end at least twice around the wires between any two three-bead loops of dark amber beads. Clip the tails on the front side of the flower.

12 Attach two of the bronze strips in the same way between the two three-bead dark amber loops on either side of the point where you attached the turquoise strip.

13 Interlace the three strips of filigree by crossing and re-crossing them over and around each other, gently pulling the motifs of each strip around in front of or behind the stems and branches of the others until the three strips are securely joined. Tweak and shape some more as needed.

14 Repeat steps 11 and 12, attaching the second turquoise strip directly opposite the first.

15 Repeat step 13.

16 Attach the clasp as explained in the Basics section on page 24, inserting all the tails before twisting.

17 Adjust the size of the bracelet by further tweaking it to shorten it or by gently stretching it to lengthen it.

faux diamond
necklace & earrings

This stunning faux diamond duo
will have you red-carpet ready.

DIMENSIONS: Necklace, 15½ inches (39.4 cm) long, plus extender chain; Earrings, ½ inch (1.3 cm) wide

necklace

▶ what you need

- Basic Tool Kit (see page 10)
- 4 yards (3.6 m) of silver 28-gauge craft wire or dead-soft sterling silver wire
- Gold lobster claw clasp
- 230 crystal AB bicone beads, 4 mm
- Gold extender chain

▶ motifs

- Five-Petal Flower, page 30
- One-Bead Single Leaf, page 32

▶ step by step

1 Cut a 3-foot (.91 m) piece of wire. Insert the wire at its center point through the loop on one side of the clasp. Twist a ¼-inch (6 mm) section of main stem.

2 On one of the wires, make a Five-Petal Flower Motif through step 2. Carrying one of the wires across behind the flower, add a bead to the other wire and rest the bead in the flower's center. Twist a ⅛-inch (3 mm) section of main stem.

3 Make a One-Bead Single-Leaf Motif on each side of the main stem. Twist a ⅛-inch (3 mm) section of main stem.

4 Repeat steps 2 and 3 twenty-eight times. Repeat step 2 once more.

5 Twist an additional 1-inch (2.5 cm) section of main stem. Add the other side of the clasp as explained on page 24, and clip the tails. Add the extender chain to the clasp.

earrings

▶ what you need

- Basic Tool Kit (see page 10)
- 1 foot (30.5 cm) of 28-gauge silver craft wire or dead-soft sterling silver wire
- 12 crystal AB bicone beads, 4 mm
- Post earrings with ⁵⁄₁₆-inch (8 mm) flat front for gluing
- Epoxy glue

▶ motif

- Five-Petal Flower, page 30

▶ step by step

1 Cut a 6-inch (15.2 cm) piece of wire. Make a Five-Petal Flower through step 3 at the wire's center point. Twist the wires at the flower's base just enough to secure the center bead in place. Tuck the final twisted section under the flower so that it lies as flat as possible. Finish off.

2 Repeat for the other earring.

3 Glue the flower motif to the front of the post earring, and let it dry.

pastel flower
chandelier *earrings*

Fresh and flirty, these alluring flower earrings
are sure to turn heads.

DIMENSIONS: 1⅞ inches (4.7 cm) long, not including ear wires

► what you need

- Basic Tool Kit (see page 10)
- 7 feet (2.13 m) of 28-gauge silver craft wire or dead-soft sterling silver wire
- 12 blue 4 mm bicone crystal beads
- 2 to 3 mm round gemstone beads or size 11° seed beads:
  - 34 green (chalcedony)
  - 16 yellow (jade)
  - 4 turquoise
- Pair of gold ear wires
- 2 gold 6 mm soldered rings, or extender chain
- 2 yellow 6 mm bicone crystal beads
- 2 gold head pins

► motifs

- Five-Petal Flower, page 30
- Six-Petal Flower, page 32

► step by step

1 Cut the wire into two 16-inch (40.6 cm) and two 26-inch (66 cm) pieces.

2 Using one of the 16-inch (40.6 cm) pieces, and using blue bicones for the petals, make a Six-Petal Flower Motif at its center point through step 2 (do not place a bead across the center). Using either one of the wires, and using green rounds for the petals and a yellow round for the center, make a complete Six-Petal Flower Motif to lie on top of the first, "tacking" it to the bottom center point of the bicone ring just before you add the center bead (see figure 1).

▲ figure 1

3 Twist a ⅛-inch (3 mm) length of main stem. Using round-nose pliers and both wires, wire-wrap a loop at the end of the stem, coiling the wires back down as close as possible to the motif.

4 Bring the wires behind the motif, going past two bicones (see figure 2). Bring the wires around and through, between the second and third petals, and pull them tight. Twist a ⅛-inch (3 mm) length of stem.

▲ figure 2

5 Repeat steps 3 and 4.

6 Repeat step 3 again. Finish off as explained in the Basics section on page 21.

7 Curve the first and third wire-wrapped loops downward somewhat (see photo).

8 Attach an ear wire to the second wire-wrapped loop made, making sure you that the flower faces forward.

9 Repeat steps 2 through 8 for the other earring.

10 Using one of the 26-inch (66 cm) pieces of wire, and using green rounds for the petals, make a Five-Petal Flower Motif at the wire's center point through step 2 (do not place a bead across the center).

11 Twist a ⅛-inch (3 mm) length of main stem. Using round-nose pliers and both wires, wire-wrap a loop at the end of the stem, coiling the wires back down as close as possible to the motif.

12 Add a yellow round to one of the wires, and carry it across the front of the flower to serve as the flower's center. Carry the unbeaded wire across, behind the flower to meet the first. Twist the shortest possible length of main stem (see figure 3).

▲ figure 3

13 Using yellow rounds for the petals, make a Five-Petal Flower Motif at the wire's center point through step 2 (do not place a bead across the center).

14 Add a turquoise round to one of the wires, and carry it across the front of the flower to serve as the flower's center. (Be sure that three of the yellow round beads lie above the wire and two below.) Carry the unbeaded wire across, behind the flower to meet the first. Twist the shortest possible length of main stem (see figure 4).

15 Using green rounds for the petals, make a Five-Petal Flower through step 2 (do not place a bead across the center).

▲ figure 4

16 Add a yellow round bead to one of the wires, and carry it across the front of the flower to serve as the flower's center. Carry the unbeaded wire across, behind the flower to meet the first. Twist a ⅛-inch (3 mm) length of main stem. Using round-nose pliers and both wires, wire-wrap a loop at the end of the stem, coiling your wires back down as close as possible to the motif (see figure 5). Finish off as explained in the Basics section on page 21.

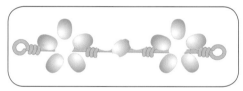

▲ figure 5

17 Using a scrap of wire, insert it between the bottom two yellow rounds, and wrap it around the wire there several times to anchor it in place (see figure 5 again). Twist a ⅛-inch (3 mm) length of stem, and wire-wrap a loop, coiling your wires back down as close as possible to the motif. Finish off as before.

18 Repeat steps 10 through 17 for the other earring.

19 Use the jump rings to attach the earring tops to the bottom strips of flowers.

20 Add a turquoise round, a 6 mm bicone, and a green round to one of the head pins. Wire-wrap it to the bottom center loop.

21 Repeat step 20 for the other earring.

red & black
tango earrings

These dramatic wire chandeliers will swing and move with you.

DIMENSIONS: 2½ inches (6.4 cm) long (not including ear wires) by ¾ inch (1.9 cm) wide

▶ what you need

- Basic Tool Kit (see page 10)
- 3 feet (.91 m) of 28-gauge black craft wire
- Size 11° seed beads:
  - 40 red
  - 52 burgundy
  - 12 black
- 20 red 3 mm fire-polished beads
- 8 red 4 mm fire-polished beads
- 10 black 3 mm black bicone crystals
- 12 black 3 mm fire-polished beads
- 10 black 4 mm fire-polished beads
- 2 black 5 x 7 mm teardrop beads
- 14 black 2-inch (5 cm) head pins
- Pair of black ear wires

▶ motif

- One-Bead Single Leaf, page 32

▶ step by step

1 Cut the wire in half.

2 Twist a loop at the center point of one piece of wire, as explained in the Basics section on page 15 (this will be the loop that you will later attach to the ear wire).

3 Add a red seed bead, a burgundy seed bead, and another red seed bead to each wire. Twist the shortest possible section of main stem (just three or four half-twists).

4 To one tail, add a red seed, a burgundy seed, a red 3 mm fire-polished bead (FP), and another red seed. Holding the first three beads down against the main stem, use the last red seed bead to make a One-Bead Single-Leaf Motif on a ⅜-inch (9.5 mm) branch (see figure 1), twisting back to the red 3 mm FP. Repeat on the other side of the earring.

5 Tweak these two branches so that they curve toward the beginning loop of the piece at their tips (see figure 2).

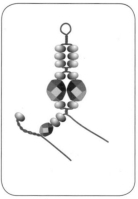

▲ figure 1

▲ figure 2

▲ figure 3

▲ figure 4

▲ figure 5

6 Add a red 4 mm FP and a black seed bead to each wire. Twist the shortest possible section of main stem.

7 To one wire add two red seed beads and three burgundy seed beads. Push the beads down to the main stem, and wrap the free end of the wire twice around the curved branch directly above it (see figure 3). Repeat with the other wire.

8 To one of the wires, add two black seed beads and one red 3 mm FP (see figure 4). Make a loop by wrapping the wire all the way around the round-nose pliers, very close to the FP and then rotating the pliers 1½ times, just as you did in step 2. You may need to back the nose of the pliers out just slightly at each half twist, since the loop will be tightening as you twist them.

9 Add another 3 mm red FP. Holding the pliers very close to it, make another wire loop. Repeat twice (see figure 5).

10 Repeat steps 8 and 9 on the other side of the earring.

11 To each wire add one 3 mm red FP. Using the two wires as one, wire-wrap a loop. Finish off.

12 Repeat steps 2 through 11 for the other earring.

13 Load the head pins with the remaining beads as indicated in figure 6, and wire-wrap them to the loops.

14 Attach the top loops of the earrings to ear wires.

▲ figure 6

tuscan gold
necklace & earrings

With rich red and gold tones aplenty,
this sultry necklace makes quite a statement.

necklace

▶ what you need

- **Basic Tool Kit** (see page 10)
- 15 feet (4.57 m) of 28-gauge burgundy craft wire or dead-soft wire
- 1 amber 7 x 10 mm crystal briolette
- 4 mm fire-polished beads:
  - 28 yellow
  - 24 magenta
  - 36 burgundy
- 26 melon 4 mm bicone crystals
- 3 mm fire-polished beads:
  - 52 dark amber
  - 48 red
- 1 gold lobster-claw clasp
- 1 gold 4 to 6 mm jump ring

▶ motifs

- One-Bead Single-Leaf Motif, page 32
- Three-Bead Single-Leaf Motif, page 33
- Seven-Bead Single-Leaf Motif, page 33

▶ step by step

1 Cut the wire into four 3½-foot (1.1 m) pieces.

2 Using half of the remaining wire, make a "hanger-style" wire wrap for your briolette as explained in the Basics section on page 25.

left center section

3 Begin the densely beaded center section of the first side of the necklace with one of the 3½-foot (1.1 m) pieces of wire. (Add wire as needed.) Add six 4 mm fire-polished beads (FP) in the following order: one yellow, one magenta, two burgundy, one magenta, and one yellow. Center them on the wire, and twist the shortest possible section of main stem (just three or four half-twists), forming them into a loop. This will be the front center section of this side of the necklace.

4 To one tail, add a bicone, an amber 3 mm FP, a red 3 mm FP, and another amber 3 mm FP. Holding the bicone down against the main stem, use the three FP to make a Three-Bead Single-Leaf Motif on a ½-inch (1.3 cm) branch (see figure 1), twisting back to the bicone. Repeat on the other side.

▲ figure 1

DIMENSIONS: 17 inches (43.2 cm) long and 1 inch (2.5 cm) wide

5 Tweak these two branches so that they curve toward the beginning loop of the piece at their tips (see photo on page 91).

6 Add a burgundy FP to each wire. Twist the shortest possible section of main stem.

▲ figure 2

7 To one wire, add a magenta 4 mm FP, a melon bicone, and a 3 mm amber FP. Push the beads down to the main stem, and wrap the free end of the wire twice around the curved branch above it on the same side of the piece (see figure 2). Repeat with the other wire.

8 To each wire, add a red 3 mm FP, an amber 3 mm FP, a magenta 4 mm FP, a burgundy 4 mm FP, and a red 3 mm FP. Bring the two wires together, and twist the shortest possible section of main stem.

9 To one wire, add a magenta 4 mm FP, a bicone, an amber 3 mm FP, a red 3 mm FP, and an amber 3 mm FP. Holding the first two beads down against the main stem, use the three FP to make a Three-Bead Single-Leaf Motif (as in step 4) on a ¼-inch (6 mm) branch, twisting back to the bicone. Repeat on the other side of the piece.

10 Repeat step 5.

11 To each wire add an amber 3 mm FP and a burgundy 4 mm FP. Bring the two wires together, and twist the shortest possible section of main stem.

12 To each wire add a yellow 4 mm FP, a magenta 4 mm FP, and a red 3 mm FP. Push the beads down to the main stem, and wrap the free end of the wire twice around the curved branch above it on the same side of the piece. Repeat with the other wire.

13 To each wire add two amber 3 mm FP, a red 3 mm FP, a bicone, and a magenta 4 mm FP. Twist a ¼-inch (6 mm) section of main stem.

▶ **The piece should now measure somewhere in the neighborhood of 2¼ inches (5.7 cm).**

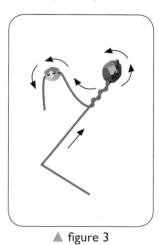

▲ figure 3

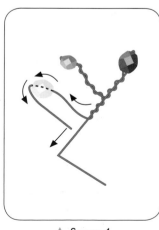

▲ figure 4

left middle section

▶ **From this point on, select the beads in random order.**

14 Make a 1½- to 2½-inch (3.8 to 6.4 cm) main branch with two or three sub-branches coming off of it at ½-inch (1.3 cm) intervals (see figures 3 and 4), with each main branch and sub-branch holding a One-Bead Single-Leaf Motif. Twist a ¼-inch (6 mm) section of main stem.

15 Repeat step 14 on the opposite side of the main stem five more times.

16 Tweak each of the six main- and sub-branches extensively, curling them around and back, toward and over, under, or even around the main stem as needed to get a very elaborate, open, lacy effect. You may want to curl them around each other at some points as well to enhance the sturdiness of this section.

▶ **The piece should now measure somewhere in the neighborhood of 3¾ inches (9.5 cm).**

left loop section

17 Make a Seven-Bead Single-Leaf Motif on a ½-inch (1.3 cm) branch. Twist a ¼-inch (6 mm) section of main stem.

18 Repeat step 17 on the opposite side of the main stem twice more.

▶ **The piece should now measure somewhere in the neighborhood of 4½ inches (11.4 cm).**

left rear section

19 Make a One-Bead Single-Leaf Motif on a 1-inch (2.5 cm) branch. Twist a ¼-inch (6 mm) section of main stem.

20 Repeat step 19 on the opposite side of the main stem.

21 Make a One-Bead Single-Leaf Motif on a ¾-inch (1.9 cm) branch. Twist a ⅜-inch (9.5 mm) section of main stem.

22 Repeat step 21 on the opposite side of the main stem.

23 Make a One-Bead Single-Leaf Motif on a ½-inch (1.3 cm) branch. Twist a ½-inch (1.3 cm) section of main stem.

24 Repeat step 23 on the opposite side of the main stem three more times or until this side of the necklace reaches 8 inches (20.3 cm) (or desired length).

25 Twist an additional 1-inch (2.5 cm) section of main stem. Tweak the branches as needed to get an attractive effect.

26 Repeat steps 3 through 25 for the other side of the necklace.

joining the two sides

27 Using the remaining short piece of wire, thread it through the center pairs of burgundy 4 mm FP from top to bottom (see figure 5). Add two magenta 4 mm FP to one of the wires. Thread the other wire through the two magenta beads from the opposite direction (see figure 6).

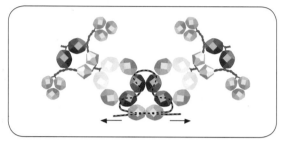

▲ figure 5

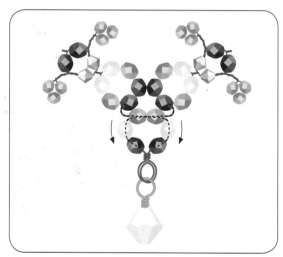

▲ figure 6

28 Add a yellow 4 mm FP and a burgundy 4 mm FP to each wire. Bring the two wires together and, using both wires as one, wire-wrap a loop into the wire-wrapped loop above the briolette. Clip tails.

29 Shape the necklace so that each side curves around to conform to the shape of your neck. Tweak as needed to fine-tune the look of the necklace.

30 Add the clasp and ring as explained in the Basics section on page 24.

earrings

▶ what you need

- **Basic Tool Kit** (see page 10)
- 2½ feet (76.2 cm) of 28-gauge burgundy craft wire or dead-soft wire
- 4 mm fire-polished beads:
  - 12 burgundy
  - 4 magenta
  - 8 yellow
- 4 mm bicone crystals:
  - 8 melon
  - 4 magenta
- 3 mm fire-polished beads:
  - 24 dark amber
  - 4 red
- 2 amber 6 mm bicone crystals
- 2 gold head pins
- Pair of gold ear wires

▶ motif

- Three-Bead Single Leaf, page 33

▶ step by step

1 Cut the wire in half.

2 Using round-nose pliers, fold one of the wires over at its center point, and twist a loop as explained in the Basics section on page 15. This will be the top loop of the earring.

3 Add a burgundy, a magenta, and a yellow 4 mm fire-polished bead (FP) to each wire. Twist the shortest possible section of the main stem (just three or four half-twists).

4 To one of the wires, add a 4 mm melon bicone, an amber 3 mm FP, a red 3 mm FP, and another amber 3 mm FP. Holding the bicone down against the main stem, use the three FP to make a Three-Bead Single-Leaf Motif on a ½-inch (1.3 cm) branch, twisting back to the bicone. Repeat on the other side of the earring.

5 Tweak these two branches so that they curve upward at their tips (see photo).

6 Add a burgundy FP to each wire. Twist the shortest possible section of the main stem.

7 To one wire add a melon bicone, a magenta bicone, and a 3 mm amber FP. Push the beads down to the main stem and wrap the free end of the wire twice around the curved branch above it on the same side of the earring (see figure 2 in the necklace instructions). Repeat for other side.

8 To each wire add two 3 mm amber FP, one burgundy 4 mm FP, one yellow 4 mm FP, and one amber 3 mm FP. Twist the shortest possible section of the main stem.

9 Using both wires as one, wire-wrap a loop. Clip the tails.

10 Using a head pin, add a 6 mm bicone and wire-wrap it to the bottom loop of the earring.

11 Attach top loop of the earring to the ear wire.

12 Repeat steps 2 through 11 for the second earring.

DIMENSIONS: 1⅞ inches (4.6 cm) long (not including ear wires) and 1 inch (2.5 cm) wide

pretty in pink **barrette**

This ab-fab accent makes any updo perfect for downtown.

DIMENSIONS: 3 inches (7.6 cm) long by 1 inch (2.5 cm) wide

▶ what you need

- **Basic Tool Kit** (see page 10)
- 3-inch (7.6 cm) barrette base
- 6 feet (1.83 m) of burgundy 28-gauge craft wire
- 4 grams each, size 11° seed beads:
  - Magenta
  - Hot pink
  - Medium pink
  - Light pink
  - Pale pink
- 6 feet (1.83 m) of hot pink or magenta 28-gauge craft wire

▶ step by step

1 Remove the flexible arched piece from the inside of the barrette.

2 Using the burgundy wire, wrap its end several times around the barrette base near the hinge end, bringing it up through the hole at the end at least twice to anchor it in place.

3 Add nine seed beads of any one color. Holding the seed beads 1 inch (2.5 cm) or so out from the barrette base, form them into a loop and give several twists to secure the loop in place. Then twist the wires back to the barrette base.

4 Coil the wire once, all the way around the base near its end.

5 Repeat step 3 twice. Coil once more around the base on the other side of the hinge.

6 Rotating the colors, repeat step 3, wrapping the wire once around the base after each twisted section, until you have about 8 inches (20.3 cm) of wire left. Wrap around on the far side of the latch on the underside of the base. (If necessary, spread the coils out by nudging them along the base to reach that point.)

7 Repeat step 3 twice more near the end of the base. Finish off by wrapping the wire several times around the base, bringing it up through the hole at least twice to secure it in place. Clip the tail.

8 Add the other wire at the end where you just finished off and repeat the whole process, working back to the other end.

9 Tweak each branch so that the loops lie more or less flat (horizontal to the flat top side of the barrette base). Reinsert the flexible, curved piece into the underside of the base.

DIMENSIONS: 7½ inches (19 cm) long

summer garden
cuff bracelet

Lightweight yet high impact, this colorful cuff bracelet is a natural choice no matter the season.

what you need

- Basic Tool Kit (see page 10)
- 14 feet (4.3 m) of 28-gauge gold-filled craft wire or dead-soft wire
- 4 mm crystal AB bicone beads:
  - 25 red
  - 25 orange
  - 20 gold
  - 14 yellow
  - 14 turquoise
- 16 inches (40.6 cm) of memory wire
- 4 inches (10.2 cm) of 20-gauge half-hard gold-filled wire

color key

Color A = Red
Color B = Orange
Color C = Gold
Color D = Yellow
Color E = Turquoise

motifs

- Five-Petal Flower, page 30
- One-Bead Single-Leaf, page 32

step by step

1 Cut a 1-yard (.91 m) piece of 28-gauge wire. Using Color A crystals for the petals and a Color D crystal for the center, begin with a Five-Petal Flower Motif. Twist a ¼-inch (6 mm) main stem.

2 Using Color E, make a One-Bead Single-Leaf Motif on a 1¼-inch (3.2 cm) branch. Twist a ¼-inch (6 mm) length of main stem.

3 Using Color B for the petals and a Color D crystal for the center, make a Five-Petal Flower Motif on a ¼-inch (6 mm) branch. Twist a ¼-inch (6 mm) length of main stem.

4 Repeat steps 2 and 3 on the opposite side of the main stem from the last leaf motif.

▶ **From this point on, rotate the colors on the flowers—i.e., C, A, B, C, A, B, etc. Add wire as needed, as explained in the Basics section on page 18.**

5 Repeat step 4 until you have used up all the crystals (14 flower motifs in all). Finish off as explained in the Basics section on page 21.

6 Using round-nose pliers, tweak the filigree strip by curving the flower motif branches all in the same direction and curling the leaf motif branches in the opposite direction (see photo on page 98). Continue until the outer edges of the flowers and the outermost curves of the leaf branches more or less line up.

7 Cut the memory wire in half. Using round-nose pliers, curl a loop at each end of both pieces. Make sure the loops are completely closed.

8 Cut a 3-foot (.91 m) piece of dead-soft wire. Leaving a ½-inch (1.3 cm) tail, attach it to the loop at one end of one piece of memory wire, as explained in the Basics section on page 20. Keep coiling tightly around the loop portion of the memory wire until it is completely covered. Continue coiling on past the loop for about ¼ inch (6 mm). See section on coiling on page 28.

9 Line up the floral strip with one of its long edges against the memory wire. Tack it in place temporarily (see Tacking Filigrees in Place on page 27), omitting the first motif.

10 Coil once into the first (next) flower motif (see Attaching Filigrees to Frames on page 27) by bringing the wire through the flower between the two petals along the outer edge of the floral strip. Continue coiling for roughly ¾ inch (1.9 cm) or so (distances between motifs may vary by ⅛ inch [3 mm] or so). Coil once or twice around the outermost curve of the next leaf motif branch. Continue coiling for ¾ inch (1.9 cm) or so.

11 Repeat step 10 until you reach the end of memory wire. Coil around the loop portion. Finish off as explained in the Basics section on page 21.

12 Using the second piece of memory wire, repeat steps 8 through 11 on the other side of the floral strip.

13 Cut the 20-gauge wire in half. Using round-nose pliers, make the end bars by curling a loop in each end of each piece. Attach the ends of the bars to the memory-wire loops at the ends of the bracelet, shortening the bars as necessary to fit the width of the bracelet itself. Squeeze the 20-gauge loops gently so that the bars are fixed firmly in place on the outer side of the bracelet.

pearl heart pendant

This striking pendant pairs gold accents and pearls for extra sizzle.

DIMENSIONS: 2 inches (5 cm) long and 1¾ inches (4.4 cm) wide

▶ what you need

- Basic Tool Kit (see page 10)
- 3½ feet (1.1 m) of 28-gauge silver craft wire or dead-soft sterling silver wire
- 40 white 2 mm pearls or size 11° pearlized seed beads
- 5 grams of size 13° or 15° gold charlottes or seed beads
- 6 inches (15.2 cm) of 20-gauge half-hard sterling wire
- 1 gold 8 mm jump ring
- 6 inches (15.2 cm) of 24-gauge gold-filled half-hard wire
- 16- to 18-inch gold-filled chain
- 2 white 3 to 4 mm pearls
- Gold lobster-claw clasp
- 1 gold 6 mm soldered ring

▶ motifs

- Five-Petal Flower, page 30
- Three-Bead Single Leaf, page 33

▶ step by step

1 Cut a 1½-foot (45.7 cm) piece of 28-gauge wire. Using 2 mm pearls for the petals and a charlotte for the center, begin with a Five-Petal Flower. Twist a ⅛ to ³⁄₁₆-inch (3 to 5 mm) main stem.

2 Using three charlottes, make a Three-Bead Single Leaf on a ⅛-inch (3 mm) branch on the right side of the main stem.

▶ **After step 2, from that point on, twist a ⅛- to ³⁄₁₆-inch (3 to 5 mm) main stem section between each motif.**

3 On the same side of the main stem, work another Five-Petal Flower Motif on a ¼-inch (6 mm) branch.

4 On the same side of the main stem, work another Three-Bead Single-Leaf Motif on a ⅛-inch (3 mm) branch.

5 On the opposite side of the main stem, work another Five-Petal Flower Motif on a ¼-inch (6 mm) branch.

6 On the opposite side of the main stem, work another Three-Bead Single-Leaf Motif on a ⅛-inch (3 mm) branch.

7 Repeat steps 3 and 6 four times more.

8 Repeat step 3. Twist an additional 2-inch (5 cm) section of main stem.

9 Bend the 20-gauge wire at a 90-degree angle at its halfway point. Curl a closed loop toward the inside of the "V" at each end, as explained in the Basics section on page 27. Gently shape the wire into a heart, making the closed loops overlap. Cut a 3-inch (7.6 cm) piece of 28-gauge wire, and wrap it several times around both ends of the wire just above the loops to hold the top of the heart closed.

10 Using the round-nose pliers, tweak the strip of filigree by gently curving the branches of the motifs. Shape the strip so that, when the first flower motif made is just to the left of the closed loops, it lies attractively all along the left-hand side of the heart and about halfway up the right-hand side (see photo on page 101). Make loops in the final 2-inch (5 cm) section of twisted wire as needed, and clip tails.

11 Using short scraps of 28-gauge wire, "tack" the filigree in place on its frame at each projected point of contact as explained in the Basics section on page 27 (see figure 1).

▶ **The points of contact may differ slightly from those in the diagram. What is important is that the filigree lies comfortably and attractively inside the frame.**

12 Cut a 2-foot (61 cm) piece of 28-gauge wire, and attach it to the frame just below the closed loop, as explained in the Basics section on page 20 (see figure 1).

13 Work down to the first point of contact by making single-charlotte loops around the outer edge of the frame. Remove the first "tacking" wire, and anchor the motif to the frame, as explained in the Basics section on page 27.

14 Continue making one-charlotte loops down to the next point of contact. Remove the tacking wire from the motif, and anchor the motif to the frame.

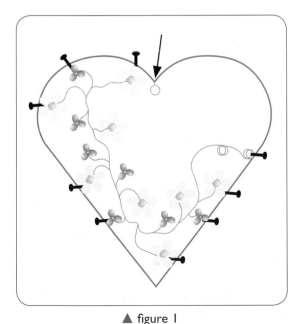

▲ figure 1

15 Repeat step 14 until all the points of contact have been anchored to the frame. Then continue looping (if there is any space left) up to the frame's closed loop. Clip tails.

16 Attach the 8 mm jump ring off center on the left-hand, top side of the heart, and close it securely.

17. Cut the 24-gauge wire in half. Wire-wrap a loop into one end of the chain, add a 3 to 4 mm pearl, and wire-wrap another loop to the clasp. Slide the chain through the 8 mm ring on the heart.

18 Wire-wrap a loop, add a 3 to 4 mm pearl, and wire another loop (as in step 17) to attach the 6 mm soldered ring on the other end of the chain.

tourmaline,
garnet & iolite
filigree earrings

Romantic hues of garnet and amethyst
sparkle in the gold wires of these elegant earrings.

DIMENSIONS: 1¾ inches (4.4 cm) long and 1¼ inches (3.2 cm) wide, not including ear wires

▶ what you need

- Basic Tool Kit (see page 10)
- 12 feet (3.7 m) of 28-gauge gold-filled craft wire or dead-soft wire
- 32 pink 2 to 3 mm faceted tourmaline rondelle beads
- 28 round 2 mm garnet beads
- 24 round 2 mm iolite beads
- 13 inches (33 cm) of 20-gauge gold-filled half-hard wire
- Pair of gold-filled ear wires
- 6 gold-filled 4 mm jump rings

▶ motifs

- Eight-Petal Flower, page 32
- One-Bead Single Leaf, page 32
- Three-Bead Single Leaf, page 33

▶ step by step

1 Cut a 1-foot (30.5 cm) piece of 28-gauge wire. Using tourmaline for the petals and a garnet for the center, make an Eight-Petal Flower Motif. Twist a ¼-inch (6 mm) section of main stem.

2 Using iolite, make a One-Bead Single-Leaf Motif on a ⅜-inch (9.5 mm) branch. Twist a ¼-inch (6 mm) section of main stem.

3 Repeat step 2 on the same side of the main stem.

4 Using garnets, make a Three-Bead Single-Leaf Motif on a ⅜-inch (9.5 mm) branch on the same side of the main stem.

5 Using iolite, make a One-Bead Single-Leaf Motif on a ⅜-inch (9.5 mm) branch on the opposite side of the main stem. Twist a ¼-inch (6 mm) section of main stem.

6 Repeat step 5.

7 Repeat step 4 on the opposite side of your main stem.

8 Repeat step 5 twice. Twist an additional 1-inch (2.5 cm) section of main stem.

9 Return to the initial tourmaline flower, and add a 10-inch (25.4 cm) piece of 28-gauge wire (see Adding New Wire on page 18). Twist a ¼-inch (6 mm) section of main stem.

10 Repeat steps 2 through 8 for the other side of the filigree, making it as close to a mirror image of the first side as possible.

11 Repeat steps 1 through 10 for the other earring.

12 Cut two 2½-inch (6.4 cm) pieces of the 20-gauge wire. Bend each wire at its center point toward the inside of the wire's natural curve (or shape the curves if needed, as explained in Shaping Frames on page 26), making a marquise shape that is slightly open at the top. Using round-nose pliers, curl a closed loop toward the back side of the frame at each end of each wire, as explained in the Basics section on page 27. This completes the inner frames.

13 Using round-nose pliers, tweak the filigrees by gently curving the branches of the motifs as shown in the photograph, shaping them as needed so that they fit around the shape of the inner frames, with the tourmaline flowers centered just under the bottom point of the frames (see Tweaking and Shaping on page 22). Curl a loop in the last 1-inch (2.5 cm) twisted section of each filigree, as close in as nec-

masquerade filigree
earrings & necklace

With undeniable grace and an air of mystery, this filigree earring and necklace set is great for a night on the town.

DIMENSIONS: 1½ inches (3.8 cm) long, not including ear wires

earrings

▶ what you need

- **Basic Tool Kit** (see page 10)
- 7 inches (17.8 cm) of 20-gauge gold half-hard wire
- 10 feet (3 m) of 28-gauge craft wire or dead-soft gold-filled wire
- Size 13° or 15° seed beads, preferably charlotte-cut:
  - 82 copper
  - 72 silver
  - 64 gold
- 68 white 3 to 4 mm freshwater pearls
- Pair of gold ear wires
- 66 head pins

▶ motifs

- Five-Petal Flower, page 30
- Three-Bead Single Leaf, page 33

▶ step by step

1 Cut the 20-gauge wire in half. Curve each wire as explained in Shaping Frames on page 26, making a bottom-heavy oval shape that is slightly open at the top. Using round-nose pliers, curl a closed loop (see Curling a Closed Loop on page 27) toward the back side of the frame at each end of each oval.

2 Cut the 28-gauge wire into two 2-foot (61 cm) pieces and two 3-foot (.9 m) pieces.

3 Using one of the 2-foot (61 cm) pieces, and using copper charlottes for the petals and a silver one for the center, make a Five-Petal Flower Motif at the center point of the wire. Twist a ¼-inch (6 mm) section of main stem.

4 Using silver charlottes, make a Three-Bead Single-Leaf Motif on a ⅜-inch (9.5 mm) branch on each side of the main stem. Add a gold charlotte to each wire, and twist a ⅜-inch (9.5 mm) section of main stem.

5 On each side of the main stem, make a main branch with two sub-branches. Using gold charlottes for the petals and copper ones for the center, make a Five-Petal Flower Motif on a ¾-inch (1.9 cm) branch, twisting only one-third of the way back toward the main stem. This is the main branch. Using silver charlottes, make a Three-Bead Single-Leaf Motif on a ⅜-inch (9.5 mm) sub-branch off the main branch (see figure 1). Twist back to the main branch. Twist a ¼-inch (6 mm) section of main branch back toward the main stem. Using copper charlottes, make another Three-Bead Single-Leaf Motif on a ⅜-inch (9.5 mm) sub-branch off the main branch (see figure 2). Twist back to the main branch. Twist the main branch the rest of the way back to the main stem. Add a silver charlotte to each wire, and twist a ⅜-inch (9.5 mm) section of main stem (see figure 3).

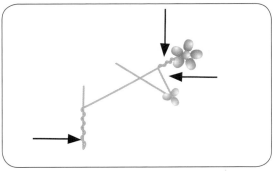

▲ figure 1

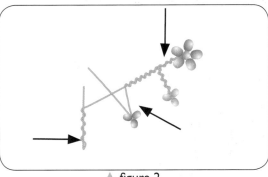

▲ figure 2

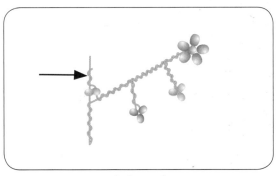

▲ figure 3

6 Using silver charlottes for the petals and gold ones for the centers, make a Five-Petal Flower Motif on a ¼-inch (6 mm) branch on each side of the main stem. Twist a ¼-inch (6 mm) section of the main stem.

7 Using copper charlottes for the petals and gold ones for the centers, make a Five-Petal Flower Motif on a ⅜-inch (9.5 mm) branch on each side of the main stem. Add a copper charlotte to each wire, and twist a ¼-inch (6 mm) section of the main stem.

8 Using gold charlottes, make a Three-Bead Single-Leaf Motif on a ¼-inch (6 mm) branch on each side of the main stem. Fasten off.

9 Repeat steps 3 through 8 for the other earring.

10 Using round-nose pliers, tweak the filigrees by gently curving the stems and branches as shown in the photograph, shaping them as needed so that they fit into the frames (see Tweaking and Shaping on page 22).

11 Using short scraps of 28-gauge wire, "tack" the filigrees in place on the frame (see Tacking Filigrees in Place on page 27) at each projected point of contact (see figure 4).

▶ **The points of contact may differ slightly from those in the diagram. What is important is that the filigree lay comfortably and attractively inside the frame.**

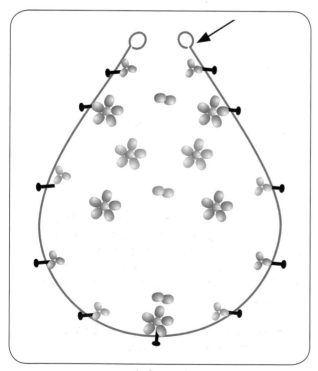

▲ figure 4

12 Using one of the 3-foot (.9 m) pieces of 28-gauge wire, attach it to the top of one frame just below the closed loop (see Adding Wire to a Frame on page 20). This is now the working wire. Coil tightly around the frame until you reach the first point of contact.

13 Remove the first "tacking" wire and coil the working wire once into the first motif (see Attaching Filigrees to Frames on page 27). Continue coiling until you reach the next point of contact.

14 Repeat step 13 until all the points of contact have been anchored to the frame. Then continue coiling up to the frame's closed loop. Clip tails.

15 Repeat steps 10 through 14 for the other earring.

16 Using a leftover scrap of 28-gauge wire, add a gold charlotte, a pearl, and another gold charlotte. Center them on the wire and bring the ends of the wire up through the loops of one of the frames, from the inside to the outside of the oval. Bring each wire around and through the frame loop again, pulling them tightly to close up the top of the frame. Add two copper charlottes to each wire. Using the two wires as one, wire-wrap a loop. Clip the tails. Repeat the process for the other earring.

17 Attach an ear wire to each loop, making sure that the flowers are facing forward.

18 Add a gold charlotte and a pearl to each of 20 head pins.

19 Wire-wrap one of the pins onto the bottom part of the hoop-loop (the coiled frame) as close as possible to the center point (on one side of the bottom copper flower).

20 Wire-wrap another pin to the loop of the previous wire wrap, placing it at the back side of the hoop-loop. Wire-wrap two more pins to that second wire-wrapped loop (again at the rear side of the hoop-loop, placing one on either side of the pearl), and then another to each of those loops. This completes the first center drop.

21 Repeat step 20 on the other side of the bottom copper flower. The second center drop is now made.

22 Repeat step 20 up through "placing one on either side of the pearl" on either side of the center drops.

23 Add a silver charlotte and a pearl to each of 12 head pins. Working outward from one side of the cluster of gold-tipped drops, repeat step 20 up through "placing it at the back side of the hoop-loop" three times. Repeat for the other side of the earring.

24 Add a copper charlotte and a pearl to each of the remaining head pins. Working outward from one side of the cluster of silver-tipped drops, repeat step 20 up through "placing it at the back side of the hoop-loop" twice. Repeat for the other side of the earring.

25 Continuing to work outward from the center, wire-wrap single head pins holding copper charlottes and single pearls until the bottom section looks full. Use any leftover head pins to fill in gaps in the fringe.

necklace

▶ what you need

- Basic Tool Kit (see page 10)
- 4 inches (10.2 cm) of 20-gauge gold half-hard wire
- 5 feet (1.5 m) of 28-gauge gold craft wire or dead-soft wire
- Size 13° or 15° seed beads, preferably charlotte-cut:
    - 39 silver
    - 32 gold
    - 45 copper
- 42 white 3 to 4 mm freshwater pearls
- 20-inch (50.8 cm) gold chain
- 21 inches (45.7 cm) of 24-gauge gold half-hard wire
- Gold lobster-claw clasp
- 1 gold soldered ring
- 33 gold head pins

▶ motif

- Three-Bead Single Leaf, page 33

▶ step by step

1 Curve the 20-gauge wire as explained in Shaping Frames on page 26, making a bottom-heavy oval shape that is slightly open at the top. Using round-nose pliers, curl a closed loop toward the back side of the frame at each end, as explained in the Basics section on page 27.

2 Cut the 28-gauge wire into one 2-foot (61 cm) piece and one 3-foot (.91 m) piece.

DIMENSIONS: 1 inch (2.5 cm) wide and 2 inches (5 cm) high, with a 20-inch (50.8 cm) chain

6 Using a short scrap of 28-gauge wire, "tack" the filigree in place on the frame (see Tacking Filigrees in Place on page 27) at each projected point of contact.

▶ **The points of contact for your filigree may differ slightly from those in the diagram. What is important is that the filigree lies comfortably and attractively inside the frame.**

7 Repeat steps 12 through 14 as for the earrings.

8 Using a leftover scrap of 28-gauge wire, add a pearl, a gold charlotte, a pearl, a gold charlotte, and another pearl. Center them on the wire, and bring the ends of the wire up through the loops of one of the frames. Bring each wire around and through the frame loop again, pulling them tightly to close up the top of the frame. Add two copper charlottes to each wire. Using the two wires as one, wire-wrap a loop. Clip the tails.

9 Cut the chain in half.

10 Cut the 24-gauge wire into five 3-inch (12.7 cm) pieces and one 6-inch (15.2 cm) piece. Using the 6-inch (15.2 cm) piece, wire-wrap a loop into the end of one piece of chain. Add a copper charlotte and a pearl. Slide the wire through the loop on the pendant. Add another pearl and another copper charlotte. Wire-wrap a loop into the end of the other piece of chain.

11 Cut each of the pieces of chain about an inch from the wire wrap. Using one of the 3-inch (7.6 cm) pieces of wire, wire-wrap a loop into the last link. Add a silver charlotte, a pearl, and another silver charlotte. Wire-wrap another loop to the end of one of the long pieces of chain. Repeat for the other side of the necklace.

12 Using one of your remaining 3-inch (7.6 cm) pieces of wire, wire-wrap a loop into the last link. Add a copper charlotte, a pearl, and another copper charlotte. Wire-wrap a loop into the clasp. Repeat on the other side of the necklace with the ring.

13 Add pearl dangles as for the earrings.

3 Work as for earrings through step 8. Do not fasten off.

4 Using silver charlottes, make a Three-Bead Single-Leaf Motif on a ¼-inch (6 mm) branch on each side of the main stem.

5 Using round-nose pliers, tweak the filigree by gently curving the stems and branches as shown in the photograph, shaping them as needed so that they fit into the frames (see Tweaking and Shaping on page 22).

butterfly pin

Let your imagination fly when composing the fiery colors of this shimmering pin.

▶ what you need

- Basic Tool Kit (see page 10)
- 16 feet (4.9 m) of 28-gauge silver craft wire or dead-soft sterling silver wire
- 4 inches (10.2 cm) of 20-gauge half-hard sterling silver wire
- 3 mm fire-polished beads: about 28 each of red, orange, yellow, and green
- 4 grams of size 15° silver metallic charlottes or seed beads
- Pin back, 1 inch (2.5 cm) long
- Strong adhesive craft glue

▶ motif

- Five-Bead Single Leaf, page 33

▶ step by step

1 To make the frame, bend the 4-inch (10.2 cm) piece of 20-gauge wire at the halfway point into a "V" shape. Curl a closed loop at each end toward the outside of the "V" shape. The loops will be the ends of the butterfly's antennae.

2 Cut a 3-foot (91.4 cm) piece of 28-gauge wire. Attach it to the frame at the bottom of the "V" as explained in the section Adding New Wire to a Frame on page 20. Continuing up one arm of the frame, make 12 tight coils.

▶ All motifs in this pattern are Five-Bead Single Leaf Motifs (as shown on page 33). To create your own unique butterfly, you can use your colors randomly or in any pattern you like.

3 Work a Five-Bead Single Leaf motif on a ⅜-inch (1 cm) branch. Moving further up, coil your wire tightly around the frame four times.

4 Continue to alternate adding motifs and coiling around the frame with the following pattern:

- Work a motif on a ½-inch (1.3 cm) branch and make five coils.
  - Work a motif on a ½-inch (1.3 cm) branch and make six coils.
    - Work a motif on a ¼-inch (6 mm) branch. (You will have completed the lower part of the butterfly's wing.) Make 20 coils.
    - Work a motif on a ½-inch (1.3 cm) branch and make five coils.

DIMENSIONS: 2¼ inches (5.7 cm) long by 2¼ inches (5.7 cm) wide

- Work a motif on a ⅝-inch (1.6 cm) branch and make five coils.
- Work a motif on a ¾-inch (1.9 cm) branch and make five coils.
- Work a motif on a 1-inch (2.5 cm) branch and make five coils.

5 To finish one side of the butterfly, work a motif on a ½-inch (1.3 cm) branch and then coil your wire all the way up to the top loop of the frame. Finish off the wire as explained in the Basics section on page 21.

6 Tweak the branches so that they curve gently as shown in the photograph, overlapping the motifs slightly as needed to get an attractive shape for the wings.

7 Attach wire to the first branch made, placing your coils around the branch as close as possible to the frame.

8 Make 6-charlotte loops around the outer edge of the lower wing (see figure 1), anchoring each loop on a branch or between beads as explained in the section Looping on Beads on page 28. Finish off.

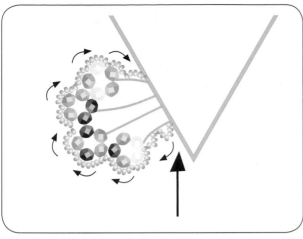

▲ figure 1

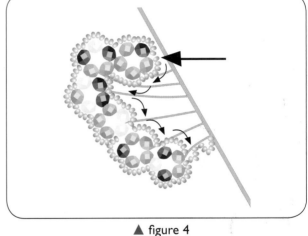

▲ figure 3

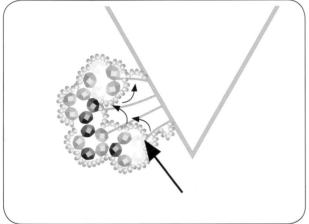

▲ figure 2

▲ figure 4

9 Re-attach wire where indicated by the arrow on figure 2. Make 6-charlotte loops along the inner edge of the beaded area of the lower wing as shown on the same diagram. Finish off.

▶ **These diagrams are meant as guides only. To achieve an attractive shape and design for the wings, you may need to add or subtract a charlotte bead—or even a whole charlotte loop—here or there. You may also need to anchor your charlotte loops in places other than those indicated by the diagrams.**

10 Make 6-charlotte loops around the outer edge of the upper wing (see figure 3), anchoring each loop on a branch or between beads as explained in the section Looping on Beads on page 28. Continue on,

making 6-charlotte loops around the inner edge of the beaded area of the upper wing (see figure 4).

11 To make the other side of the butterfly, repeat steps 2 to 10 on the other side of the frame.

12 Gently bend the frame inward at its bottom point to bring the two sides closer together. Cut a 2-inch (5 cm) piece of wire and coil it five times around both arms of the frame just below the top beaded section of the butterfly. Finish off at the back of the pin.

13 Glue the pin back securely to the back of the pin, placing it perpendicular to the frame and hiding it behind the top beaded section. Let the glue dry for 48 hours before wearing the piece.

red crystal cluster ring

This red-hot ring packs its share of crystal sparkle, and then some.

► what you need

- Basic Tool Kit (see page 10)
- Ring mandrel
- Metal file
- 10 feet (3.1 m) of 28-gauge black craft wire
- 1 foot (30.5 cm) of 22-gauge silver half-hard wire
- 100 red 3 mm fire-polished beads

► step by step

1 Using round-nose pliers, curl a loop at one end of the 22-gauge wire. Using chain-nose pliers, continue curling the wire into a flat spiral about ½-inch (1.3 cm) wide at its widest point (see figure 1).

▲ figure 1

▲ figure 2

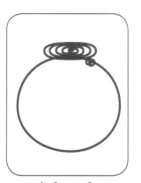

▲ figure 3

▲ figure 4

2 Bend the working wire out at a 90-angle from the spiral. Use the ring mandrel to start curling it under the spiral into a band about one size larger than the size you want to end up with, bringing the wire around past the spiral on its flatter side (see figure 2).

► **The ring size will shrink some as you apply the loops of beads and as you coil around the band.**

3 Coil the working wire twice around the ring band as close as possible to the spiral at the point where you bent the wire away from the spiral to form the right angle (see figure 3), checking frequently to make sure the band size stays the same.

4 Bring the wire around again to double the ring band. Do not pass the spiral this time. Instead, checking again to make sure the two loops of the ring band are remaining equal and the same size as before, coil the working wire around the ring band right up against the near side of the spiral (see figure 4).

DIMENSIONS: 1½ inches (3.8 cm) high and 1 inch (2.5 cm) wide

5 Clip the tail at the front side of the ring, and file the end, if required.

6 Using 1 yard (.91 m) or so of 28-gauge wire, secure it to the inner point of the spiral by wrapping it tightly around there three times.

7 Add three beads. Holding them about ¼-inch (6 mm) out from the spiral—⅜-inch (9.5 mm) if you want a more lavishly sized ring ornament—form them into a loop and twist back to the spiral. Wrap the wire around the spiral twice to secure the first loop of beads in place.

8 Working outward around and around the spiral, keep adding loops of beads as in step 7 until you have covered the entire spiral and the ring looks full. (Add wire as necessary.) Finish off.

▶ **You can slide the loops along the rounds of the spiral, if needed, to bring them closer together or farther apart.**

9 Tweak as necessary to get a nice dome shape.

10 Join the remaining piece of 28-gauge wire to the ring band as close as possible to one side of the spiral. Note: Treat both loops of the band as one.

11 Coil the 28-gauge wire tightly around the ring band, as explained in the Basics section on page 28.

12 When you have covered the entire band, clip the tails on the outer side of the ring, and press them flat.

DIMENSIONS: Tiara, 12½ (31.8 cm) long and 1 inch (2.5 cm) wide; Cuff Bracelet, 7½ inches (19 cm) long and 1 inch (2.5 cm) wide

crystal
wedding set

More is more with this shimmering crystal wedding set.

tiara/choker

▶ what you need

- Basic Tool Kit (see page 10)
- 16 feet (4.9 m) of 28-gauge gold-filled craft wire or dead-soft wire
- 4 mm bicone crystals:
  - 27 crystal AB
  - 11 beige
- 2 pieces of gold memory-choker wire, for tiara or small choker, 13 inches (33 cm) each

  or
- 2 pieces of gold memory-choker wire for medium choker, 14 inches (35.6 cm) each
- 2 pieces of gold memory-choker wire for large choker, 15 inches (38.1 cm) each
- 4¼ inches (10.8 cm) of 20-gauge half-hard gold-fill wire
- 10 grams of size 15° crystal AB seed beads

▶ motifs

- Five-Petal Flower Motif with Beaded Outline, page 30
- One-Bead Single-Leaf Motif with Beaded Outline, page 34

▶ step by step

center section

1 Cut a 10-inch (25.4 cm) piece of 28-gauge wire. Using crystal AB for the petals and beige for the center, make a Five-Petal Flower Motif with Beaded Outline.

2 Twist a ⅝-inch (1.6 cm) section of main stem.

3 Using crystal AB, make a One-Bead Single-Leaf Motif with Beaded Outline on a ⅜- to ½-inch (9.5 mm to 1.3 cm) branch. Twist a ¼-inch (6 mm) section of main stem.

4 Using beige, repeat step 3 on the opposite side of the main stem twice. Finish off after the second motif.

5 Return to the initial flower motif, and add an 8-inch (20.3 cm) piece of 28-gauge wire at its center point in the same spot where the first stem is attached (see Adding New Wire on page 18). Twist a ⅝-inch (1.6 cm) section of main stem.

6 Repeat steps 2 through 4 for the other side of the filigree, making it as close to a mirror image of the first side as possible.

7 Bend both of the pieces of memory wire downward just slightly at their center points (*not* with the natural curve—see figure 1), as explained in the Basics section on page 26. Curl closed loops downward at each end on one piece and upward on the other.

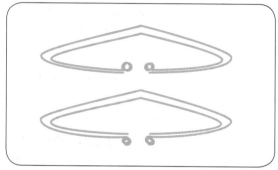

▲ figure 1

8 Using round-nose pliers, tweak both filigrees by gently curving the branches of the motifs, as shown in the diagrams, shaping them as needed so that they fit along the shape of the frame as explained in the Basics section on page 26. Finish off.

9 Cut the 20-gauge wire into two ¼-inch (3.2 cm) pieces and two ⅞-inch (2.2 cm) pieces. Using round-nose pliers, curl a small closed loop at both ends of each piece. This completes the struts. Set aside.

10 Using short scraps of 28-gauge wire, "tack" the filigree in place at each projected point of contact on the piece of memory wire that has the up-turned loops, as explained in the Basics section on page 27 (see figure 2).

▶ **The points of contact may differ slightly from those in the diagram. What is important is that the filigree lay comfortably and attractively inside the frame.**

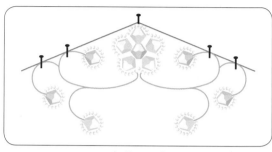

▲ figure 2

11 Cut a 2-foot (61 cm) length of 28-gauge wire, and attach it to the frame (see figure 2), as explained in the Basics section on page 20. This will be the upper frame if you will be using the piece as a tiara (the lower frame if it is to be a choker).

12 Work over to the next point of contact by making single-seed bead loops around the outer edge of the frame as explained in the Basics section on page 28, except that you will be making three unbeaded wraps between each loop instead of one. Remove the tacking wire from the motif, and anchor the motif to the frame, as explained in the Basics section on anchoring wires on page 27.

13 Repeat step 12 until all points of contact have been anchored to the frame. Then repeat the number of single-seed bead loops you made before the first tack. Finish off.

14 Attach the two longer struts to the frame at the beginning and ending points (see figure 3), making sure that the open sides of the loops are toward the back. Attach their other ends to the lower frame in the same manner. Line the upper and lower frames up so that their ends meet at their closed loops. Wrap scraps of 28-gauge wire six or seven times around both frames just prior to the loops to secure the final shape of the frame.

15 Tack the filigree to struts and lower frame (see figure 3 again).

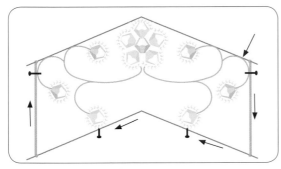

▲ figure 3

16 Continue looping on beads and anchoring motifs to the struts and frame until this entire section has been outlined with single-seed bead loops. Finish off.

side sections

17 Cut a 15-inch (38.1 cm) piece of 28-gauge wire. Using crystal AB for the petals and beige for the center, make a Five-Petal Flower Motif with Beaded Outline as above. Twist a ¼-inch (6 mm) section of main stem.

18 Using crystal AB, make a One-Bead Single-Leaf Motif with Beaded Outline as above on a ⅜-inch (9.5 mm) branch. Twist a ⅜-inch (9.5 mm) section of main stem.

19 Repeat step 18 on the same side of the main stem. Twist a ½-inch (1.3 cm) section of main stem.

20 Using beige, repeat step 18 on the opposite side of the main stem. Twist a ⅜-inch (9.5 mm) section of main stem.

21 Repeat step 18 on the opposite side of the main stem. Twist a ⅜-inch (9.5 mm) section of main stem.

22 Repeat step 18. Twist an additional 1 inch (2.5 cm) of main stem, and finish off.

23 Repeat steps 17 through 22 for the other middle side-section. Flip the flower over to get a mirror image.

24 Tweak and shape the filigrees as shown in figure 4.

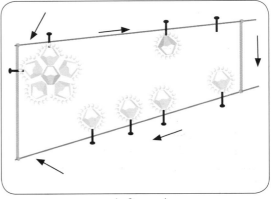

▲ figure 4

25 Attach the shorter struts to the upper and lower frames as above.

▶ **If the struts are too long for the shape of the frame, simply clip off a bit of the closed loops at one end or the other, and curl the loop down farther before attaching it to the frame.**

26 Tack the filigrees to the frame, and then attach them in the same manner as above (see figure 4 again). Note that the "tacks" on the longer struts will be permanent ones. Finish off.

outer end sections

27 Cut a 6-inch (15.2 cm) piece of 28-gauge wire. Using crystal AB, make a One-Bead Single-Leaf Motif with Beaded Outline as above. Twist a 3-inch (7.6 cm) section of main stem.

28 Tweak and shape the filigree, making three loops in the twisted portion of main stem as shown in figure 5.

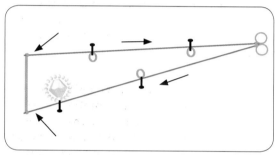

▲ figure 5

29 Repeat steps 27 and 28 for other outer end section.

30 Tack the filigrees to the frame, and then attach them in the same manner as above (see figure 5 again). Finish off.

DIMENSIONS: 1½ inches (3.8 cm) long (not including ear wires) and 1¼ inches (3.1 cm) at widest point

earrings

▶ what you need

- Basic Tool Kit (see page 10)
- 5 feet (1.5 m) of 28-gauge gold-filled craft wire or dead-soft
- 4 mm bicone crystals:
  - 16 crystal AB
  - 6 beige
- 7 inches (17.8 cm) of 20-gauge half-hard gold-filled wire
- 10 grams of AB size 15° crystal seed beads
- Pair of gold ear wires

▶ motifs

- Five-Petal Flower Motif with Beaded Outline, page 30
- One-Bead Single-Leaf Motif with Beaded Outline, page 34

► step by step

1 Cut an 8-inch (20.3 cm) piece of 28-gauge wire. Using crystal AB for the petals and beige for the center, make a Five-Petal Flower Motif with Beaded Outline.

2 Twist a ½-inch (1.3 cm) section of main stem.

3 Using beige, make a One-Bead Single-Leaf Motif with Beaded Outline on a ½-inch (1.3 cm) branch on each side of the main stem (do *not* twist a section of main stem in between them). Finish off.

4 Repeat steps 1 through 3 for the other earring, making it as close to a mirror image of the first side as possible.

5 Cut the 20-gauge wire in half. Bend one piece to a 90° angle at its center point, and then again along each side 1½ inches (3.8 cm) from the center bend, as explained in the Basics section on page 26 (see photo). Curl closed loops toward the center opening at each end. This completes the frame. Repeat for the other earring.

6 Using round-nose pliers, tweak the filigrees by gently curving the two leaf branches downward, shaping them as needed so that they fit into the frame.

7 Using short scraps of 28-gauge wire, "tack" the filigree in place at each projected point of contact on the frames (i.e., the outer side of each leaf motif and the center points of the second and fourth petals of the flower), as explained in the Basics section on page 27.

8 Cut a 1½-foot (45.7 cm) length of 28-gauge wire, and attach it to the frame next to one of the closed loops, as explained in the Basics section on page 20.

9 Work down to the first (next) point of contact by making single-seed bead loops around the outer edge of the frame, as explained in the Basics section on page 28, except that you will be making three unbeaded wraps between each loop instead of one. Remove the tacking wire from the motif, and anchor the motif to the frame.

10 Repeat step 9 until all points of contact have been anchored to the frame. Then repeat the number of single-seed bead loops you made before the first tack. Finish off.

► **If the frame is larger than needed, clip a small portion at a time from the closed loops, and re-curl them until the frames are the optimal size for the filigree, uncoiling one or more single-seed bead loops if necessary.**

11 Repeat steps 6 through 10 for the other earring.

12 Cut the remaining 28-gauge wire into six pieces.

13 Wire-wrap a loop at one end of one piece, add a crystal AB, and wire-wrap another loop. Attach one of these loops to one of the top loops of the frame. Repeat for the other side of the frame.

14 Repeat step 13 for the other earring.

15 Using one of the remaining pieces of 28-gauge wire, add a crystal AB. Thread the tails of wire through the top wire-wrapped loops of an earring. Add two seed beads to each tail. Bring the tails together and, treating the two wires as one, wire-wrap a loop. Attach this loop to the ear wire. Repeat for the other earring.

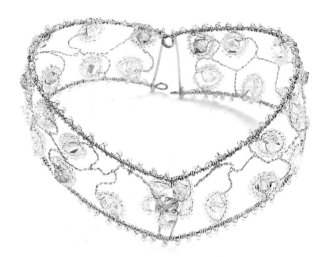

cuff bracelet

▶ what you need

- Basic Tool Kit (see page 10)
- 12 feet (3.7 m) of 28-gauge gold-filled craft wire or dead-soft wire
- 4 mm bicone crystals:
  - 21 crystal AB
  - 9 beige
- 2 inches (5 cm) of 20-gauge half-hard gold-filled wire
- 2 pieces of gold memory-bracelet wire, 8 inches (20.3 cm) each
- 10 grams of size 15° crystal AB seed beads

▶ motifs

- Five-Petal Flower Motif with Beaded Outline, page 32
- One-Bead Single-Leaf Motif with Beaded Outline, page 34

▶ step by step

1 Cut a 2½-foot (76.2 cm) piece of 28-gauge wire. You will need to later add wire as necessary. Using crystal AB for the petals and beige for the center, make a Five-Petal Flower Motif with Beaded Outline.

2 Twist a ⅝-inch (1.6 cm) section of main stem.

3 Using crystal AB, make a One-Bead Single-Leaf Motif with Beaded Outline on a ⅜- to ½-inch (9.5 mm to 1.3 cm) branch. Twist a ⅜-inch (9.5 mm) section of main stem.

4 Repeat step 3 on the opposite side of the main stem.

5 Using beige, repeat step 3 on the opposite side of the main stem.

6 Repeat step 3 twice and then step 5. Repeat this three times.

7 Repeat the first part of step 3 (up to "Twist"). Finish off.

8 Return to the initial flower motif, and add a 24-inch (61 cm) piece of 28-gauge wire across from the spot where the first stem is attached (see Adding New Wire on page 18).

9 Repeat steps 2 through 7 for the other side of the filigree, making it as close to a mirror image of the first side as possible.

10 Bend both of the pieces of memory wire downward just slightly at their center points (*not* with the natural curve—see figure 1 from the necklace instructions) as explained in the Basics section on page 26. Curl closed loops at each end of each wire. This completes the frames.

11 Using round-nose pliers, tweak the filigree strip by gently curving the branches of the motifs toward the center on one side of the strip of filigree and away from the center on the other, shaping them as needed so that they fit along the shape of the frame.

12 Cut the 20-gauge wire into two 1-inch (2.5 cm) pieces. Using round-nose pliers, curl a small closed loop at each end of each piece. This completes the struts. Set aside.

13 Using short scraps of 28-gauge wire, "tack" the upper edge of the filigree in place at each projected point of contact (i.e., the outer side of each leaf motif and the center point of the flower) on one frame as explained in the Basics section on page 27 (see figure 6). This will be a bit more difficult on the bracelet than on the necklace, since the strip is longer and the curve of the bent memory wire necessitates that you constantly renegotiate with the filigree to make it lie flat.

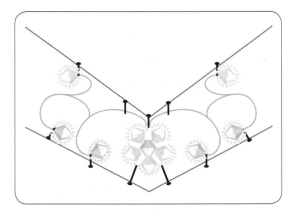

▲ figure 6

14 Cut a 3-foot (.91 m) length of 28-gauge wire, and attach it to the frame next to the closed loop at one end, as explained in the Basics section on page 20.

15 Work your way over to the first (next) point of contact by making single seed-bead loops around the outer edge of the frame, as explained in the Basics section on page 28, except that you will be making three unbeaded wraps between each loop instead of one. Remove the tacking wire from the motif, and anchor the motif to the frame, as explained in the Basics section on page 28.

16 Repeat step 15 until all the points of contact have been anchored to the frame. Then repeat the number of single seed-bead loops you made before the first tack. Finish off.

17 Attach the struts to the frame next to the closed loops, making sure that the open sides of the loops are toward the back. Attach their other ends to the lower frame in the same manner.

18 Tack the filigree to the lower frame (see figure 6 again). Do not tack the flower.

19 Loop on beads and anchor motifs to the struts and frame by making single seed-bead loops up to the flower. The bottom of the flower will not touch the bottom frame, nor does it have a center point that is accessible for attaching. Simply attach it on both sides of its center bead with a looser loop of wire to allow for the extra space between the flower and the frame. Continue looping on beads to the end of the frame. Finish off.

gauge chart

▲ the brown and sharp (b. & s.) gauge for wire and sheet metal

gauge number	thickness in inches	thickness in millimeters
3/0	.409	10.388
2/0	.364	9.24
1/0	.324	8.23
1	.289	7.338
2	.257	6.527
3	.229	5.808
4	.204	5.18
5	.181	4.59
6	.162	4.11
7	.144	3.66
8	.128	3.24
9	.114	2.89
10	.101	2.565
11	.090	2.28
12	.080	2.03
13	.071	1.79
14	.064	1.625
15	.057	1.447
16	.050	1.27
17	.045	1.114
18	.040	1.016
19	.035	.889
20	.031	.787
21	.028	.711
22	.025	.635
23	.022	.558
24	.020	.508
25	.017	.431
26	.015	.381
27	.014	.376
28	.012	.304
29	.011	.29
30	.01	.254
31	.008	.203
32	.0079	.199
33	.007	.177
34	.006	.152
35	.0055	.142
36	.005	.127

acknowledgments

I would like to thank both of the editors who worked on this book: Jane LaFerla for all her work and patience early in the process, and Larry Shea who really hit the ground running in the third quarter. My thanks also to the many people at Lark Books who contributed to the accuracy and beauty of *Boutique Bead & Wire Jewelry:* Megan Kirby (art director), Travis Medford (associate art director), Jeff Hamilton and Shannon Yokeley (art production assistance), Marthe Le Van (senior editor), and Mark Bloom (editorial assistance). And thanks to Stewart O'Shields and Steve Mann (photographers), Megan Cox (photography assistant), and Val Anderson (proofreader). Together, you've made a lifelong dream of mine come true.

index